TH
DISSERTATION DESK REFERENCE

THE DOCTORAL STUDENT'S MANUAL
to Writing the Dissertation

RAYMOND L. CALABRESE

ROWMAN & LITTLEFIELD EDUCATION
Lanham • New York • Toronto • Plymouth, UK

Published in the United States of America
by Rowman & Littlefield Education
A Division of Rowman & Littlefield Publishers, Inc.
A wholly owned subsidiary of The Rowman & Littlefield Publishing Group, Inc.
4501 Forbes Boulevard, Suite 200, Lanham, Maryland 20706
www.rowmaneducation.com

Estover Road
Plymouth PL6 7PY
United Kingdom

British Library Cataloguing in Publication Information Available

Library of Congress Cataloging-in-Publication Data

Calabrese, Raymond L., 1942–
The dissertation desk reference : the doctoral student's manual to writing the dissertation / Raymond L. Calabrese.
p. cm.
Includes bibliographical references.
ISBN 978-1-60709-473-9 (cloth : alk. paper) —
ISBN 978-1-60709-474-6 (pbk. : alk. paper) —
ISBN 978-1-60709-475-3 (electronic)
1. Dissertations, Academic—Handbooks, manuals, etc. 2. Report writing—Handbooks, manuals, etc. 3. Academic writing—Handbooks, manuals, etc. I. Title.
LB2369.C273 2009
808'.02—dc22 2009026554

Manufactured in the United States of America.

To Babe, my inspiration, love, and friend.

CONTENTS

ACKNOWLEDGMENTS

The Dissertation Desk Reference is in print because hundreds of doctoral students and their advisors collaborated on producing a dissertation that met the highest standards of academic scrutiny at their institutions. The confidence expressed by the doctoral student and his or her university to publish the dissertation as an electronic thesis or dissertation (ETD) and make it accessible to the global academic community deserves recognition and applause. Without their contribution, examples within *The Dissertation Desk Reference* would not be possible.

I acknowledge the friendship and confidence that my editor, Dr. Thomas Koerner, placed in my ideas for another dissertation book. Tom asked important questions at the outset that shaped the direction of the book. I want to acknowledge Dr. Sally J. Zepeda, professor at the University of Georgia (Athens). Dr. Zepeda is a long-time friend and colleague who supported my work with a staunch belief that it makes a difference in the lives of students and practitioners. Dr. Zepeda's unselfish gift of time in reviewing my manuscript, providing suggestions to improve content and readability, is an exemplar for university faculty. I also wish to acknowledge Dr. Jon Engelhardt, dean of the School of Education at Baylor University, a long-time friend and mentor, who shared his understanding of doctoral education and current practices for this project. I thank Dr. Bill Phillips, dean of the College of Education at Eastern Kentucky University, for recognizing the value this book creates for doctoral students. I also wish to acknowledge Dr. Patti Chance, Educational Leadership department chair at San Diego State University, for providing sound dissertation advising expertise that helped to shape my ideas.

INTRODUCTION

As I recall my personal journey to earn my doctoral degree, I remember classes, meeting with professors, and discussions of heady ideas. It was a grand time—until it was time to write the dissertation! Metaphorically, I was on my own to unlock the door to the kingdom of completed dissertations. I tried hundreds of keys in thousands of doors until I found the correct key that fit into the dissertation door. I discovered that the dissertation process was one of endurance, will-power, and patience. During most of this journey, I felt alone—a solitary traveler. I later discovered that thousands of others made a similar journey. I learned the road to writing the dissertation is a mystery for most doctoral candidates.

As a professor who guides doctoral students, I did not want my doctoral students to travel the same road. I wanted them to spend time on conducting a quality study that made a difference in society. I encouraged them to spend their time communicating the results of their studies to the members of their committee and university community, then to the academic world through publication and presentation of their studies. I speculated with regard to what kind of questions I would have to ask to change my students' dissertation experience.

I learned through my research that if you want a different answer, you ask a different question. I began to ask different questions. How can I demystify the dissertation process? What do students need to know to facilitate the dissertation-writing process? What can I do so students would not have to reinvent the dissertation-writing wheel? The answer was immediate and simple: Provide students with a blueprint devoid of academic rhetoric that provides a plan to bore a hole through the dissertation mountain. The result was *The Elements of an Effective Dissertation and Thesis: A Step-By-Step Guide to Getting It Right the First Time.* I witnessed this book providing a jump-start for my students. I also heard from other doctoral students and professors who expressed how it provided a plan to bore the hole through the dissertation mountain.

I felt there was more I could do, however, to assist in the dissertation process. I asked a new question: What is the next phase beyond *The Elements of an Effective Dissertation* that would simplify the dissertation-writing process? The answer to this question was to provide a user-friendly book that was an easy and immediate reference for doctoral students and the professors who chair dissertation committees. I also wanted this user-friendly book to provide knowledge, examples, and models from completed dissertations. *The Dissertation Desk Reference* represents my continued efforts to simplify the dissertation-writing process for doctoral students and their major professors.

I began working on *The Dissertation Desk Reference* by researching hundreds of dissertations and identifying their main components. Simply stated, the doctoral student's discipline does not alter the primary components of a dissertation. Dissertations differ by discipline in format, presentation, and content. Yet the global nature of the dissertation is similar.

From my research, I harvested the components that consistently appear in dissertations. I prepared a separate entry for each component and placed each one in alphabetic order. This was the first step: a dictionary dissertation desk reference for doctoral students. Yet, I felt there was more I could do. I added a suggestion of where the component might be found in a traditional, five-chapter dissertation. I took a further step and provided a comprehensive example taken directly from a high-quality dissertation for each component. I accompanied each example with a note describing what the researcher did in the example. I concluded each component with a checklist.

I believe that doctoral students and their faculty advisors will find this book user-friendly. If the doctoral student, for example, feels overwhelmed or frustrated when writing a problem statement, she or he simply opens *The Dissertation Desk Reference* to the Ps, finds *problem statement*, reads the definition, identifies the part of the dissertation where it is commonly found, reviews an example, and applies the checklist to his or her dissertation. The student does not reinvent the dissertation-wheel; she or he uses the example as a model from which to develop that part of the dissertation. The faculty advisor can use *The Dissertation Desk Reference* to point the doctoral student in the right direction.

The book includes 150 components and an equal number of examples coupled with suggestions for placement and a checklist to guide the doctoral student's dissertation. The doctoral student can now concentrate on conducting and reporting a quality study.

A few notes for the reader to maximize readability: (1) All components are alphabetized. (2) Where I identified different wording for a component, for example *analysis of data* and *data analysis* or *Chapter 1* and *introductory chapter*, I arbitrarily selected one, and referenced the other entry to the defined entry.

A

ABSTRACT

The abstract of the dissertation briefly describes the research you conducted for your study. The abstract also allows the reader to identify the level of interest in reading the dissertation. A good dissertation abstract is composed of five key components: (1) *statement of the purpose* or *problem statement;* (2) the *research questions* and *hypotheses;* (3) description of the *methodology,* which includes *study design, participants, data sources,* and *processes;* (4) *findings,* devoid of the discussion narrative; and (5) the study's *implications.* Use key words central to the study in the abstract to facilitate database searches for researchers following a similar line of inquiry.

> The abstract is located prior to the introductory chapter and after the acknowledgments.

Example

In this example, the researcher begins the abstract with a direct statement of the purpose of the study. The researcher concludes the abstract with a direct statement of the implications of the study.

Abstract

> Using variables from two specific strands within the body of educational research, that is, economic theory and organizational theory, a series of hypotheses and a set of theoretical models of student achievement were developed and tested.

Student Instructional Ratio (SIR) and Student Services Ratio (SSR), measures of fiscal efficiency, were the variables selected from the economic literature base. Collective efficacy of teachers, teachers' perceptions that the efforts of the faculty as a whole will have a positive influence on students, represented the organizational variable. In addition to these variables, socioeconomic status (SES) and prior student achievement were included in the study as control variables.

The theoretical models advanced within the study predicted that SIR as well as SSR had an indirect effect on student achievement through the collective efficacy of teachers. To test these models, data were collected from 146 elementary schools within the state of Ohio. Correlational analysis and structural equation modeling techniques were employed to analyze the data and determine the validity of the models.

The results of this investigation failed to support the hypotheses that SIR or SSR had an indirect effect on student achievement through the collective efficacy of teachers. However, collective efficacy of teachers was found to have a positive, direct effect on student achievement, controlling for both SES and prior student achievement. Not surprisingly, evidence from the data analyses showed SES to be directly related to student achievement and indirectly related to student achievement through the collective efficacy of teachers. The importance of collective efficacy in facilitating student achievement was demonstrated by the research.

The absence of finding a significant relationship between fiscal efficiency and student achievement through the key process variable of the collective efficacy of teachers precipitated *ex post facto* analyses on the sample set. These exploratory analyses demonstrated that money allocated directly to the instructional process at the school did have a significant, indirect effect on student achievement through the collective efficacy of teachers. Taken together, these results prompted the presentation of numerous implications for theory, practice, and future research. (Cybulski, 2003, pp. ii–iii)

Abstract Checklist

- ☐ Include the five key components of your study in the abstract.
- ☐ State each of the five key components succinctly.
- ☐ Provide sufficient information to the reader to understand what occurred in the study.
- ☐ Use key words central to the study to facilitate database searches.

ACKNOWLEDGMENTS

The acknowledgment page is an expression of your gratitude to people who supported, encouraged, taught, and coached you on the doctoral journey. The acknowledgments should begin with the chair and other members of your committee. Next, the researcher recognizes the study's participants and those responsible at the site of the study for approving the conduct of the study. The researcher also recognizes those who made intellectual, technological, or labor-intensive contributions to your dissertation: (1) faculty not serving on your committee; (2) reviewers of surveys or questionnaires, protocols, methodology; (3) those who provided inspiration through their writing or lectures, students, administrative assistants, technical support; and (4) family and friends.

A well-written acknowledgment page is generous in praise, moving well beyond simple expressions of thanks. The researcher specifically identifies the person's contribution to you and its connection to the finished product—the dissertation.

> The acknowledgment page is located at the beginning of the dissertation just prior to the table of contents. In some cases, it is the first entry after the table of contents.

Example

In this example, the researcher begins the acknowledgments with a tribute to the researcher's chair and committee.

Acknowledgments

I am especially grateful to my Dissertation Director/Committee Member, Dr. Charlene A. Trovato, for her belief in my desire to allow students' voices to be heard. Her advice and direction throughout the study process was much appreciated. I would also like to express appreciation to my Dissertation Mentor/Committee Member, Dr. Charles J. Gorman. He encouraged me with positive messages and insight that kept me focused and moving forward. Dr. Gorman was patient, compassionate, and instrumental in this educational journey.

Appreciation is extended to my committee members, Dr. Jacqueline M. Respress and Dr. Richard Seckinger. Their valuable time, suggestions, and guidance throughout the process was greatly appreciated. Additionally, there was much support and assistance received from friends and family in order to complete this study in its entirety. I thank Dr. Martha Diamond for her perceptivity, advice, and selfless dedication to my work. She understood my challenges and navigated me through the most difficult of times.

Heartfelt thanks are given to my parents, Anthony and Fannie Galmarini for their belief in me and understanding that learning is a lifetime venture. They continue to be a constant source of support no matter what my endeavors. As first-generation Americans, I thank them for their modeling of good work ethics, values, integrity, and commitment to one another. I recognize my mother-in-law, Connie Mangino, who encouraged me in my decision to continue my education and who has made sacrifices on my behalf. I also dedicate this study to my late father-in-law, Thomas M. Mangino, who instilled selflessness, compassion, and forward-thinking in his son, my husband. My love is extended to my twins, Mark and Melina, who at the age of two were patient, understanding, and inquisitive about my educational trek. . . . Last but not least, I am indebted to my husband, Matthew. Without his support for the past twenty years, I am certain I would not have reached this level in my education. . . . (Mangino, 2008, pp. xi–xii)

Acknowledgments Checklist

- ☐ Recognize each person who contributed to the completion of the dissertation in the acknowledgments.
- ☐ Give generous praise to those named in the acknowledgments.
- ☐ Describe the specific contribution of each person in the acknowledgments.

ANALYSIS (QUALITATIVE)

The description of qualitative analysis procedures is an important part of the researcher's dissertation. The researcher describes the qualitative analysis procedures used to analyze data. The researcher clearly describes the unit of analysis. She or he identifies any assumptions that were taken to the analysis, and identifies how categories for the placement of data (e.g., from the literature, emerging from data collection) were selected.

The researcher identifies the coding scheme used in the study. She or he may also include the coding scheme in the *appendices*. The researcher uses precise language to describe how she or he applied pattern matching, content analysis, and any application of text or analysis software used to code, identify themes, and determine findings. Moreover, the researcher describes how she or he prepared data for analysis through the processes and procedures used to examine, categorize, tabulate, and synthesize or test data (Yin, 2003).

> The analysis (qualitative) is located in the methodology or the results chapter.

Example

In this example, the researcher describes the process and strategies used for analysis of qualitative data collected in this study.

Data Analysis (Qualitative)

> I began the initial analysis process by "reading" the narratives during the very first week of data collection. During this phase of analysis I began to "read" or "listen" to the data that had been collected (Maxwell, 2005). This "rough" analysis gave me the opportunity to write notes regarding what I saw and/or heard initially in the data. I began to develop tentative ideas regarding relationships and categories. This "rough" analysis also served to simulate the analytical thinking process that guided the categorizing and connecting strategies.
>
> This analytical process included exploring the data for individual metaphors, experiences, and chronologies, and included comparing and contrasting patterns in the form of a collective voice. I looked for patterns within their narratives. After this "rough" analysis, I began the formal phase of data analysis on both individual and collective levels by using the constant comparative method (LeCompte & Preissle, 1992). This method assumes "that the data collection and analysis are recursive, one informing the other throughout the course of the study" (Howard, 2003, p.7). As Merriam (1998) asserts, this involves comparing one segment of a narrative from different data collection modes (i.e., interviews, observations, or

> researcher notes) to another segment of a narrative within the same or different data collection mode. This formal analysis phase of data analysis is also referred to as coding (Maxwell, 2005). (Seagraves, 2007, pp. 108–109)

Analysis (Qualitative) Checklist

- ☐ Provide a comprehensive description of data analysis procedures used in the study.
- ☐ Provide a clear understanding of qualitative analysis procedures with citations.
- ☐ Describe the application of data analysis software.

ANALYSIS (QUANTITATIVE)

The description of quantitative analysis procedures is an important part of the researcher's dissertation. The description of analysis requires the researcher to describe (1) how she or he prepared the data for analysis, how the researcher ascertained that the data were accurate, and what procedures the researcher used, including software used to analyze the data; (2) a detailed account of the study's sample and the measures used in the study (if human beings were involved in the study, the researcher provides demographic data and descriptive statistics related to the sample); and (3) a detailed account of the statistical model used to assess the study's hypotheses (Trochim, 2006). The researcher provides tables and figures in this section and refers to them in the description of analysis.

> The analysis (quantitative) is located in the results chapter.

Example

In this example, the researcher identifies the statistical methods used to analyze data. See *statistical methods* for an additional example.

Data Analysis (Quantitative)

> The research questions in this study were examined using the Statistical Package in Social Science (SPSS) software. Summary descriptive statistics

> were computed for the demographic portions of the instrument as well as the dependent and independent variables examined in this study. Means, standard deviations, and ranges of scores on the factored subscales were reported for the total sample of schools. (Clark, 2005)

Analysis (Quantitative) Checklist

- ☐ Provide evidence of the accuracy of data collected.
- ☐ Provide a detailed description of the study's sample.
- ☐ Describe the demographics of the sample.
- ☐ Provide descriptive statistics related to the sample.
- ☐ Describe the statistical procedures used to assess measures used to test the study's hypotheses.
- ☐ Provide tables and figures.

ANCILLARY FINDINGS

Ancillary findings are also labeled *unexpected findings* or *incidental findings.* Ancillary findings are distinguished from initial findings, as they are a surprise or epiphany to the researcher. As a result of the ancillary findings, some researchers may perform additional analysis or research. Ancillary findings are reported under a separate header in the dissertation.

> The ancillary findings are located in the results chapter.

Example

In this example, the researcher describes a set of findings that the researcher did not consider major findings, but believed were worthy of note.

> ***Ancillary Findings***
>
> There were a few observations of a non-statistical nature that warrant mention at this time. The demographic information was exceptionally homogenous among the two library types. In spite of a slow return rate among ARL respondents during the start of the survey request process, more than half of those individuals who were queried responded during the third

> mailing. The breakdown of demographic information for education levels and years in the current position was also very similar. These results did provide for valid and reliable application of the statistical tests used in this study. Additionally, obtaining a response rate of 53% allowed for a strong sample of ARL and non-ARL respondents. (Brooks, 2007, p. 84)

Ancillary Findings Checklist

- ☐ Describe additional data analysis driven by initial findings in the ancillary findings section.
- ☐ Identify the processes used in any additional analysis in ancillary findings.
- ☐ Report unexpected findings under an ancillary findings section.
- ☐ Report ancillary findings in the results chapter.

ANNOTATED BIBLIOGRAPHY (see Bibliography)

APPENDICES/APPENDIX

Dissertations contain an appendices or appendix section to incorporate supportive materials related to the researcher's study. These additional materials provide deeper understanding of the dissertation, but are found at the end of the dissertation to avoid interruptions in the flow of reading the contents. The researcher, for example, may use a questionnaire as a data-gathering instrument. The first time the researcher refers to the questionnaire, she or he indicates that the questionnaire is in the appendix. The researcher appropriately labels its location in the text of the dissertation.

If the researcher uses more than one source of supportive material, the title for the section is called *Appendices.* Different materials need to be in separate sections labeled as appendices and must be referred to in the body of the dissertation. In the following example, the researcher used an e-mail correspondence letter (Appendix E) in the research study. Each piece of supportive material is generally labeled *Appendix A, Appendix B, Appendix C,* and so on; however, some departments may use numerical indicators instead of letter indicators. The materials included in the *appendices* vary.

The following list includes examples of materials taken from appendices from completed dissertations in the United States.

1. Advisor request, permissions for study
2. Block scheduling literature matrix
3. Coding categories
4. Contact summary form
5. Content classification study processes
6. Data analysis codes
7. Data-collection guidelines
8. Data matrix
9. Descriptive statistical tables
10. Educational technology survey
11. E-mail to participants
12. Final school reports
13. Informed consent form
14. Institutional Review Board (IRB) for human subjects approval
15. Instrument usability
16. Interview protocol
17. Interviewee's letter
18. Introductory letter to participants
19. Item content listing
20. Kindergarten schedules
21. Letter to superintendents
22. Member checks
23. List of urban school districts
24. Permission from superintendents
25. Postcard to participants
26. Participant interview questions
27. Raw sample data
28. Review of feedback from pilot study
29. Revised questionnaire
30. Study information sheet
31. Survey instrument
32. Survey letter for first mailing
33. Thank-you letter
34. Usability letter
35. Validity feedback form

The appendices are located at the end of the dissertation.

Example

Appendix E

The following e-mail correspondence letter was sent to all seven of the identified non-traditional superintendents as listed with the Council of the Great City Schools (CGCS). The initial correspondences were made approximately one month prior to the National Fall Conference of the CGCS in Nashville, Tennessee.

Dear Mr. (Superintendent Name),

I am writing to invite you to participate in a research study of the non-traditional superintendents of the Council of the Great City Schools. As one of the non-traditional superintendents, you are in a unique position to contribute to the knowledge base of what constitutes excellence in district-level school leadership. The focus of the study is to examine the leadership styles and characteristics of the CGCS's non-traditional superintendents. Specific objectives include examining the career paths, preparation, and work histories of the non-traditional superintendents of the Council of the Great City Schools. I hope you will agree to participate in a brief personal interview with me. I plan on attending the National Fall Conference of the CGCS in Nashville during the last week of October. I would like to arrange a time that we could meet and talk during your time in Nashville. If you are not planning on attending, I would like to arrange a telephone interview with you at your convenience. This study has human subject's approval from North Carolina State University's Institutional Review Board and Dr. Robert Carlson's support from the Council of the Great City Schools. I sincerely hope you will consider participating in this important study. I will contact you later this week by telephone to discuss your possible participation and answer any questions you may have.

Thank you,
[Name omitted](Duckworth, 2008)

Appendices Checklist

- ☐ The appendices are alphabetical and placed at the end of the dissertation.
- ☐ The appendices contain all pertinent supplemental materials integral to the study, such as *IRB* materials, questionnaires, surveys, study pro-

tocols, letters to participants, and interview questions. These supportive materials need to be in a separate section labeled *Appendices*. In this case, the appendices would read: Institutional Review Board (Appendix A), questionnaire (Appendix B), survey (Appendix C), study protocol (Appendix D), letter to participants (Appendix E), and interview questions (Appendix F).

APPROVAL PAGE

The approval page is the formal document signed by representatives of the university. The signed approval page indicates that the dissertation met all required standards for awarding the doctoral degree. It signifies that a faculty committee guided, reviewed, and tested the researcher regarding the veracity of the dissertation and the researcher's ability to communicate his or her research to a public audience. Each university and its graduate school have unique protocols indicating university sanction. As a rule of thumb, the approval page contains the signatures of the chair of the dissertation committee and committee members. Some universities require the additional signatures of the academic dean of the unit granting the degree, and the dean of the graduate school.

The approval page is located at the beginning of the dissertation just after the title page. Depending on the university, the approval page is not numbered or given a lower case Roman numeral.

Example

Approval Page (Sumner, 2006)

I am submitting herewith a dissertation written by Myrna Gail Sumner entitled "Climate and Student Performance in Tennessee Middle Schools." I have examined the final electronic copy of this dissertation for form and content and recommend that it be accepted in partial fulfillment of the requirements for the degree of Doctor of Education, with a major in Educational Administration and Policy Studies.

Gerald C. Ubben
Major Professor

We have read this dissertation
and recommend its acceptance.

E. Grady Bogue
Ernest W. Brewer
Gregory C. Petty

Accepted for the Council:
Anne Mayhew
Vice Chancellor and
Dean of Graduate Studies

(Original signatures are on file with official student records.)

Approval Page Checklist:

- ☐ Follow university and departmental protocol in formatting the approval page.
- ☐ The approval page has all appropriate signatures.
- ☐ Place the approval page in the designated place in the dissertation with appropriate page numbering.
- ☐ The signed approval page is submitted to appropriate governing bodies even if an electronic dissertation is used and does not require a formal signed document.

ARCHIVES AND ARTIFACTS

Archival material and relevant artifacts are commonly found in the *appendices.* A list of these materials is also placed in the *appendices.* Examples of archival materials or artifacts are digital photographs, sample materials, lists, or suitable documents.

> Examples of archives and artifacts are located in the appendices.

Example

In this example, the researcher describes the use of archives and artifacts as data sources.

Archives and Artifacts

> Archival documents and artifacts also contributed an aspect to data collection. Patton (2002) noted that such documentation can "provide a behind-the-scenes look at program processes and how they came into being" (p. 294). McMillan and Schumacher (2001) highlighted the use of artifacts as a supplementary technique to help interpret, elaborate on, or corroborate data obtained from the participants. Data created during the life of the special-education PAC that supported the research questions or interview findings were incorporated into the overall data analysis. Items such as special education PAC website page views, meeting minutes, supporting documentation of issues covered, electronic mailings, and other evidence supportive of the findings were used. These supporting documents were not difficult to gather, though I did need to sanitize a few (to maintain participant confidentiality) before using them whole or quoting parts of them. (Romancnuk, 2006, p. 109)

Archives and Artifacts Checklist

- ☐ Place relevant archive and artifact materials in the *appendices.*
- ☐ Create a list of archive and artifact materials placed in the *appendices* for easy reference.

ASSUMPTIONS

All empirical research has underlying assumptions embedded within that determine the direction and type of inquiry (Myers, 1997). These assumptions are speculative and untested. The researcher makes assumptions that guide the research and choice of data-gathering methods known to the reader so the reader will understand how the researcher's assumptions influence the research. The reader will then be able to make more informed decisions as to the validity of the researcher's conclusions (Engel & Schutt, 2005). The dissertation has a specific place for the researcher to state assumptions explicitly, generally in the *introductory chapter,* and often repeated in the *methodology chapter.* The researcher, by explicitly stating assumptions, informs the reader of the theory and perspective that the research is taking throughout the line of inquiry.

> The assumptions are located in the introductory chapter to the dissertation.

Example

In this example, the researcher provides the reader with assumptions made concerning the study. The researcher's assumptions are theories applied to the study.

> #### *Assumptions*
>
> CHSM students can make meaningful contributions regarding the way they learn and are taught (San Martin, 2008).
>
> Sergeants and patrol officers will honestly respond to all questions posed in the Emotional Quotient Inventory (EQ-i) test instrument (Burnette, 2006).
>
> The researcher assumed that the responses, though reflective of diverse individual respondents, would provide for a collective reflection of the practices of current public school principals. (Clinesmith, 2007)

Assumptions Checklist

- ☐ The assumptions are speculative.
- ☐ The assumptions are linked to the conclusions to allow the reader to test the *validity* of the conclusions.
- ☐ The assumptions indicate the direction of the inquiry and selected *research methods.*

B

BACKGROUND OF THE STUDY

The background of the study outlines the study for the reader of the dissertation. The background of the study provides an overview of the rationale for the choice of topic and line of inquiry in the dissertation. The primary purpose of this section is to establish the context for the problem that the researcher plans to investigate. Some dissertation formats present the background of the study as a central part of the *introduction* to the *introductory chapter.* Other formats place the background of the study as a stand-alone section in the *introductory chapter.*

The background of the study has five broad purposes: (1) to describe the background leading to inquiry into the problem identified by the researcher, (2) to offer a critical examination of the existing research into the problem, (3) to suggest unresolved issues in the established line of inquiry, (4) to communicate the importance of additional inquiry to the reader, and (5) to provide the foundational support for more extensive elaboration in the *problem statement* (Office of Behavioral and Social Sciences Research, 2001).

> The background of the study is located in the introductory chapter prior to the problem statement.

Example

In this example, the researcher uses the background of the study to illustrate the lack of empirical research in the researcher's line of inquiry.

Background of the Study

More than ever, our future depends on education. The twenty-first-century world is one of rapidly changing technology, globalization of product and financial markets, and significant demographic shifts. The workplace of tomorrow—information-intense and technologically advanced—will offer an abundance of better jobs that could bring prosperity to thousands of Americans (Jenkins, 2003).

This demographic shift is significant because, as Kelly (2005) pointed out, there are currently very large disparities in educational attainment between Whites and most minority groups. For example, between 1990 and 2000, 40% of the White U.S. population, aged 25–64, had an Associate's Degree or higher, as compared to only 15% for the Hispanic population. When looking at a Bachelor's Degree or higher, these percentages change to 30% and 10% respectively (Kelly, 2005).

Unfortunately, while an average of just over 500,000 Americans do earn a GED each year (GED Testing Service, 2005), less than one third of these individuals enroll in postsecondary education (Reder, 2007). During the past five years, this issue of low transition rates of GED recipients to postsecondary education has become a national focus.

Unfortunately, there is a paucity of research looking specifically at the GED-recipient population so the question remains if indeed GED holders enroll at high rates into remedial courses, why is their overall persistence rate so much lower than other student populations? (Sanders, 2008)

Background of the Study Checklist

- ☐ The background of the study defines the general context of the study.
- ☐ The background of the study describes the background leading to inquiry into the problem identified by the researcher.
- ☐ The background of the study provides the historical context to the research and offers a critical examination of the existing research into the problem.
- ☐ The background of the study describes substantive unresolved issues.
- ☐ The background of the study makes the case that the inquiry is substantive.
- ☐ The background of the study provides the foundational support for more extensive elaboration in the *problem statement.*

BIAS (also Researcher Bias)

The researcher describes how she or he carefully and rigorously limited the potential of researcher bias and preserved researcher neutrality during the design of the study, the conduct of the study, data analysis, and reporting of the results of the study. The researcher enhances the credibility of the study by the maintenance of neutrality. The researcher demonstrates how she or he mitigated any potential for bias. The researcher describes how she or he did not have a predetermined agenda to prove a perspective, knowingly to manipulate data, or to select only supportive data. The researcher uses a reflexive process by identifying and reporting the conditions that may lead to bias or be construed by others as having the potential to influence the researcher's study (Patton, 2002).

> The researcher bias section is located in the methodology chapter.

Example

In this example, the researcher describes the safeguards taken to reduce researcher bias.

Researcher Bias

> Researcher bias was reduced through review of all data by an experienced researcher to substantiate credibility and consistency. Additional safeguards designed to lessen the influence of personal biases on this study included systematic coding of data within and across cases, identified protocols for the study, and triangulation of data. (Thompson, 2007, p. 120)

Bias (Researcher) Checklist

- ☐ Describe how researcher bias was limited.
- ☐ Identify potential conditions that might increase researcher bias.
- ☐ Describe how data collection procedures, multiple sources of data, triangulation of data, and external review of the study prevented researcher bias (Patton, 2002).

BIBLIOGRAPHY (also References and Annotated Bibliography)

The bibliography in the dissertation is a compilation of all sources used in your research. Some universities use the term *bibliography* and *references* interchangeably to signify the sources cited in the dissertation. In the purest sense, *bibliography* refers to *all* sources, including those suggested for deeper background elaboration. The researcher provides a list of all material that informed the researcher, regardless of a source's citation within the dissertation (Gibaldi, 2003). In some cases, a university may require an annotated bibliography. An annotated bibliography refers to all of the sources used in the research. Each source is accompanied by a brief annotation that describes and critiques the source (Engle, Blumenthal, & Cosgrave, 2008).

> The bibliography typically is located at end of the dissertation. In some universities, bibliographies are located at the end of each chapter.

Bibliography Checklist

- ☐ The bibliography refers to all sources used in the research for the study.
- ☐ The references in the bibliography refer to the sources cited within the dissertation.
- ☐ Follow the stylistic guidelines set by the graduate school and department in writing the bibliography.

C

CHAPTER 1 (also Introductory Chapter)

Chapter 1 is the blueprint for the traditional dissertation. This introductory chapter prepares the reader for what is forthcoming as the researcher unfolds the story of his or her study. It also serves as an anchor as the researcher continually refers to Chapter 1 throughout the writing of the dissertation, ensuring alignment with each forthcoming component of the dissertation. Chapter 1 has the following organizational schema with its accompanying components. The definition and description of Chapter 1 components are found alphabetically in this book.

- Introduction
- Problem statement
- Purpose statement
- Overview of the methodology
- Units of analysis
- Research questions
- Identification of assumptions
- Statement of the study's objectives and aims
- Acknowledgment of limitations
- Acknowledgment of delimitations
- The significance of the study
- Definition of key terms
- Summary statement

Chapter 1 Checklist

☐ Each component listed previously is found in Chapter 1.
☐ Chapter 1 provides a blueprint for the dissertation.

- ☐ Accurately report the relevant Chapter 1 components in the appropriate places in the dissertation (e.g., the *research questions* and *hypotheses* are reported in the *methodology* and *results chapters*).

CHAPTER 2 (also Literature Review Chapter)

Chapter 2 in the traditional dissertation is the host of what many refer to as the *literature review.* The function of Chapter 2, or the literature review, is to frame the researcher's study, to link it to the antecedents with the line of inquiry (Burke, 2001), and to serve as a direct and unambiguous link to the researcher's study (Berger & Patchener, 1988). Chapter 2 links several components that contribute to the reader's deeper understanding of the study. In Chapter 2, the researcher reviews and critiques relevant literature, establishes a conceptual framework, presents the theoretical frameworks for the study, and reviews and critiques relevant empirical research. In this sense, the term *literature review* links the crucial theoretical and empirical precedents of the study. Later in the dissertation, the researcher includes discussion of his or her findings with that of the literature and research presented in Chapter 2.

Chapter 2 has the following organizational schema with its accompanying components. The definition and description of Chapter 2 components are in this book.

- Introduction
- Conceptual framework
- Theoretical perspective(s)
- Alternative or competing theories
- Empirical research search criteria
- Findings of the search for empirical research
- Review of the relevant empirical research
- Summary of chapter

Chapter 2 Checklist

- ☐ Present each component listed previously in Chapter 2.
- ☐ Provide a substantive presentation of the theoretical perspectives and relevant empirical research.

- ☐ Refer to the theoretical perspectives and relevant empirical research in the *discussion* section of the dissertation—typically, the final chapter of the dissertation.

CHAPTER 3 (also Methodology Chapter)

The researcher describes the study's methodology in Chapter 3 of a traditional dissertation. Chapter 3 has a rich descriptive nature, with the intention that the reader may fully understand the processes and procedures undertaken by the researcher. By providing this type of detail, the reader may replicate the researcher's study. The researcher presents the research design and the rationale for the design, clearly stating the theoretical research perspective that guides the methodology. The methodology section provides comprehensive descriptions of the unit of analysis and methods, including a description of the procedures used with the unit of analysis.

The researcher also describes data collection processes, efforts to reduce bias and ensure reliability, trustworthiness, and validity of the data and the data analysis procedures described in *Chapter 1*. As a result of the researcher's descriptions, the reader can ascertain the validity of the researcher's findings and conclusions (Bangert-Drowns, 2008).

Chapter 3 has the following organizational schema with its accompanying components. The definition and description of Chapter 3 components are in this book.

- Introduction
- Research design
- Methodology
- Purpose of the study
- Research questions
- Context
- Units of analysis
- Role of the researcher
- Researcher bias
- Methods
- Data analysis
- Research quality
- Summary of chapter

Chapter 3 Checklist

- ☐ Present each component listed previously in Chapter 3.
- ☐ Provide a substantive description of the methodology, research design, and data analysis.
- ☐ Describe how research quality was ensured.

CHAPTER 4 (also Results Chapter)

The researcher presents the results or findings of the study in Chapter 4 of the traditional dissertation. Ambiguity exists in this area, as different graduate schools and departments have their own norms regarding the heading of this chapter; many do not distinguish between *results* and *findings,* and use the terms interchangeably—the researcher should be clear with regard to the advisor's guidelines and departmental norms. In general, quantitative studies use the term *results* and qualitative researchers use the term *findings.* In simple terms, the researcher describes what was found in the study in Chapter 4. The results and findings are presented based on the data analysis in the order of the research questions or hypotheses stated by the researcher. The research questions or hypotheses are re-stated at the beginning of this chapter. They are replicated exactly from *Chapter 1* or *Chapter 3.* The results are presented in a straightforward manner without interpretation. The accurate presentation of the results is an expression of the researcher's integrity and ethical values. Tables and figures are presented in close proximity to the report of results for the reader to gain a clearer understanding of the reported results.

Chapter 4 has the following organizational schema with its accompanying components. The definition and description of Chapter 4 components are in this book:

- Introduction
- Restatement of the purpose of the study
- Restatement of the theoretical perspective(s)
- Restatement of the research questions/hypotheses
- Summary of results and findings
- Results presented in order of the research questions/hypotheses
- Chapter summary

Chapter 4 Checklist

- ☐ Present each component listed previously in Chapter 4.
- ☐ The results and findings presented in Chapter 4 accurately describe the research outcomes.

CHAPTER 5 (also Discussion Chapter)

The researcher presents a discussion of the *results* and *findings* in Chapter 5. The discussion chapter links all parts of the dissertation and provides the researcher's perspective on the research. The researcher's discussion is an interpretation of the *results* and *findings.* The researcher offers a subjective and speculative interpretation of causes and implications of the *results* and *findings.* In doing so, the researcher discusses the rationale for a *result* or *finding,* its *implication* on and *recommendations* for praxis, future research, and new theory. The researcher also acknowledges the study's shortcomings as well as the study's significance. She or he provides suggestions for future research to the reader in Chapter 5 (Skelton & Edwards, 2000).

- Introduction
- Restatement of the purpose of the study
- Summary of the literature review
- Summary of the methodology
- Restatement of the research questions
- Summary of findings
- Discussion of findings
- Implication for future research
- Implications for praxis and recommendations
- Relationship of findings to relevant theory
- Significance of the study
- Summary and conclusions

Chapter 5 Checklist

- ☐ Present each component listed previously in Chapter 5.
- ☐ The discussion section in Chapter 5 is an interpretative response of the results or findings presented in *Chapter 4,* and is not a replication of the *results* or *findings.*

- ☐ The conclusion section is a strong statement concerning the study's outcomes.

CHAPTER INTRODUCTION

Each chapter of the dissertation requires an introduction. The function of the introduction is similar throughout the dissertation with one important difference: In *Chapter 1*, the introduction introduces the researcher's topic to the reader. In many cases, the introduction to *Chapter 1* provides the background of the research topic that sets the stage for the problem statement.

In the remaining chapters, the introduction provides the chapter's purpose. The introduction identifies the purpose of the chapter by providing an organizational schema for the reader. The introduction also succinctly lists the core areas the researcher addresses in the chapter. The following are examples of the introduction to *Chapters 2, 3, 4,* and *5* from the traditional five-chapter dissertation.

Example

Introduction—Chapter 2

> Chapter 2 of the proposal is the literature review. It is composed of the (1) conceptual framework, (2) epistemology, (3) descriptions of the theoretical framework, (4) competing perspective, (5) a methodology for inclusion of related research in the review of the empirical literature, and (6) a synthesis of the reviewed empirical literature as it relates to minority parents who display sustained engagement or involvement in their child's education. (Sheppard, 2007, p. 19)

Example

Introduction—Chapter 3

> Chapter 3 provides the research methodology that includes the research design, methods, and data analysis. I organize this chapter with a description of the research design and methodology. I then restate the purpose of the study and research questions that will direct my study.

I follow with a description of the context, unit of analysis, role of the researcher and facilitator of an AI Learning Team process. Next, I explain my data collection methods, data analysis techniques, and research quality. I conclude with a summary of my methodology. (Glasgow, 2008, p. 44)

Example

Introduction–Chapter 4

Chapter 4 is organized first by restating the purpose of my study and describing the theoretical perspective used to guide my study. Then I present the research design and methodology and restate the research questions. Next, I detail the data analysis and summarize the findings from my study. I then include a report of findings with two sections. The first section addresses the findings by detailing the two days of the AI learning team process. The second section presents the results of each of the four findings where the participants' narrative texts are used to support the findings that emerged from the data. I conclude Chapter 4 with a summary. (San Martin, 2008, p. 54)

Example

Introduction–Chapter 5

In my final chapter, I review the purpose of the study, research questions, summary of the conceptual framework, literature review, methodology, six salient findings of the study, and discussion of the findings. I then make recommendations for future research. The chapter concludes with contributions to the profession, contributions to practice, and conclusions. (Niles, 2006, p. 109)

Introduction Checklist

- ☐ Provide an introduction to each chapter.
- ☐ Introduce the focus of the inquiry in the introduction to *Chapter 1.*
- ☐ Identify the purpose of the chapter and provide a schema for the reader in the introduction to the remaining chapters.

CHAPTER SUMMARY

A chapter summary often appears at the conclusion of all chapters. Often, the chapter summary in the final chapter of the dissertation is titled *conclusions* (See *conclusions* for a complete definition). The chapter summary provides an executive summary of the researcher's work in the chapter. The researcher succinctly includes all of the salient points in the chapter. The researcher is careful not to elaborate or to provide any extraneous material in the chapter summary. In effect, the researcher's chapter summary restates the chapter's key points allowing the reader to gain a quick understanding of what was described in the chapter.

> The chapter summary is located at the end of each chapter in the dissertation.

Example

Summary–Chapter 1

Chapter One has described the focus of the present study to be the *school variables* as having an independent influence on academic performance of students at risk of academic failure. Chapter Two follows with information on related literature in which the current study is grounded. Among other issues, the various socio-psychological variables about teaching and learning will be explored, and, by so doing, the bases for subsequent chapters will be delineated. (Chirume, 2008, p. 41)

Example

Summary–Chapter 2

Research within the past fifteen years has consistently reported higher gains for full-day kindergarten programs. The six studies that have been featured in this literature review (Cryan et al. [1992], Elicker and Mathur [1997], Hough and Bryde [1996], Morrow et al. [1998], Weiss and Offenberg [2003], and Walston and West [2004]) all concluded that full-day kindergarten does yield positive benefits for children. In summary, the increase in the instructional day does increase the number of minutes that a child is immersed in language. These studies suggest that the longer kindergarten day leads to an increase in academic achievement and an increase in desired social behaviors. This supports the premise of the theoretical framework for this study, Vygotsky's sociocultural learning theory: language acquisition increases the propensity to learn and learning continues to promote the development of the whole child. (McIntosh, 2006, p. 29)

Example

Summary—Chapter 3

The methodology of this research study was an action research using seven individual cases. As an action research project, the research team worked together to identify barriers and create units of study to implement that were considered the action piece of the study. This chapter contained the research design, setting, participants, and general results.

Chapter 4 contains a description of each case in detail. Each case study contains an introduction to history of the case, a description of each participants' classroom, and their viewpoints from each interview. Chapter 5 describes the results when each case is compared for common views and analyzed using the *National Science Education Standards* for science teaching. It also provides the findings and recommendations for further research on this topic. (Roberts, 2006, pp. 50–51)

Example

Summary—Chapter 4

Martsolf and Mickley's (1998) model was shown to be relevant and helpful tool for content analysis of transcripts from participants turning to spirituality as a response to sexual violence. The theory developed in this study extends the Martsolf and Mickley model to an integrated and dynamic process. Martsolf and Mickley's conceptual definition model functioned as a heuristic tool to initiate analysis of a complex process of using spirituality as a response to sexual violence. By initially analyzing all transcripts, then selecting fifty spiritually intense transcripts from which to extract the theory, it was possible to develop a scientifically rigorous

> theory of a social process by which participants use spirituality in response to sexual violence.
>
> A model of the theory was generated incorporating three dimensions: first, spiritual connection (communion, passion, perpetuity, presence); second, spiritual journey (being sustained, being awakened, being tested); and third, spiritual transformation (transcendence, transformative meaning). A core category of "Being Delivered" was found in the participants' transcripts. Being delivered reflects participants' use of spirituality to help them heal from the many types of sequelae of sexual violence. (Knapik, 2006, p. 81)

See *conclusions* in this book for the example of a chapter summary for Chapter 5.

Chapter Summary Checklist

- ☐ Each chapter includes a chapter summary.
- ☐ Chapter summaries are executive summaries of the chapter.
- ☐ Chapter summaries provide the salient points from the chapter in succinct format.

CLOSING THOUGHTS (see Conclusions)

CONCEPTUAL FRAMEWORK

The conceptual framework represents the researcher's thinking regarding the approach she or he will take to the study. The researcher provides an underlying model of the issue she or he is studying. This underlying model is often referred to as the *conceptual framework* (Jarvelin & Wilson, 2003). The conceptual framework acts as a vehicle to describe the background for how the researcher conceptualizes the study (Krumme, 2000). The researcher provides a summary of his or her *relevant experience* that informs the underlying models that shaped the thinking regarding the approach to the study. The conceptual framework also provides a chance for the researcher to describe his or her theoretical perspectives and how the theoretical perspectives influence the study's methodology.

> The conceptual framework is located in the introductory chapter. It may also be a part of the literature review chapter.

Example

Conceptual Framework

This study contends that several variables may be antecedents for organizational commitment. As Meyer and Allen (1997) point out, a person becomes committed to an organization for many reasons, and it is the combination of the individual's affective, continuance, and normative commitments that makes up a complete picture of commitment to the organization. The influence of the perceived level of organizational politics, the perceived level of organizational support, the structure of the organization, and the global satisfaction of the individual may have a direct affect on that person's overall commitment. This study will attempt to determine how and to what extent politics, support, structure, and satisfaction influence the three types of commitment in Meyer and Allen's (1997) conceptualization.

This study will examine the influence of two additional factors identified in the literature as having a possible impact on organizational commitment. The factor of middle manager status is a construct of student affairs professionals who report to a Chief Student Affairs Officer or other senior administrator, have worked in the profession a minimum of five years, and supervise at least one full-time student affairs professional. The work/non-work interaction factor is a construct that will explore the influence of gender, marital status, and dependent children under the age of 18 living in the respondent's home. Figure 1 illustrates the conceptual model to be used in the present study.

This study will utilize the conceptualization of perceived organizational politics (POP) proposed by Kacmar and Ferris (1991). Support will be examined using Eisenberger and associates (1986) model of perceived organizational support (POS). The theoretical underpinning for the conceptualization of organizational structure comes from the work of Burns and Stalker (1961), while the conceptualization of global job satisfaction proposed for this study will be the one developed by Ironson, Smith, Brannick, Gibson, and Paul (1989). (Boehman, 2006, pp. 16–17)

Conceptual Framework Checklist

- ☐ The conceptual framework describes the underlying model of how the researcher chose to study the topic.
- ☐ The conceptual framework identifies the theoretical perspectives and theoretical research perspectives.
- ☐ The conceptual framework describes how relevant experience informs the researcher's underlying model.

CONCLUDING REMARKS (see Conclusions)

CONCLUSIONS

The conclusions section generally appears in the last chapter of the dissertation. The researcher accurately draws conclusions from the *data analysis* and *results* and *findings*. The researcher also informs the reader what she or he did in the study. The researcher then succinctly describes the *methodology* and *theoretical perspectives* used in the study. The *methodology* provides a brief description of the *research design, units of analysis,* and *methods.* The researcher then details the *results* and *findings* from the study—accurately restating them from the *results* or *findings* chapter. Flowing out of the *results* or *findings,* the researcher describes how the *results* or *findings* add to existing research; the impact, if any, on praxis; and concludes with a definitive statement of the study's outcome. The researcher may suggest future lines of inquiry generated by the *results* or *findings* in the study as well as suggest alternative conclusions—conclusions that she or he did not expect to find in the study (Hughes, 2001).

> The conclusion is located at the end of the last chapter of the dissertation. Often the conclusion replaces the chapter summary in the last chapter.

Example

In this example, the researcher begins by restating the purpose of the study. The researcher then draws conclusions from the researcher's findings that stress the importance of the findings in application and contribution to the new knowledge.

Conclusions

> The purpose of this study was to explore the socialization experiences of full-time tenured and tenure-track African American male faculty at HBCUs and PWIs and to bring attention to their unique experiences in academia. Thompson and Dey (1998) remind us that we should focus on each individual population in the professoriate as a means for understanding their unique experiences. In this study, I examined the experiences of a subgroup of the professoriate that has been under-researched. The findings of this study indicated the experiences of African American males in the academy were not only unique, but were both rewarding and challenging simultaneously.
>
> While it is important to recognize there are similarities in the socialization experiences of all faculty, the race and gender of the participants in this study distinctly affected their socialization into the academy. For participants at the HBCUs, their race and gender often positively affected their experiences. Participants at the PWIs revealed that their race and gender not only adversely affected their experiences, but that race was a factor in all aspects of their experiences in the academy.
>
> This study contributed to the literature on faculty socialization by exploring the experiences of African American male faculty at HBCUs and PWIs. Senior faculty and administrators can use the findings of this study to enhance their understanding of the unique experiences of African American male faculty and to improve the socialization process for this particular subgroup of the professoriate. Finally, prospective African American male faculty can use the findings of this study to gain insight as to what they may experience in the academy. (McCoy, 2006, p. 130)

Conclusions Checklist

- ☐ Conclusions are accurate.
- ☐ Conclusions reiterate the study's *methodology.*
- ☐ Conclusions include the *research design, units of analysis,* and *methods.*
- ☐ Conclusions describe how the *results* or *findings* add to existing empirical research.

- ☐ Conclusions end with a definitive statement of the study's *outcome.*
- ☐ Conclusions often replace the *chapter summary* in the last chapter.

CONFOUNDING FACTORS

A confounding factor is a variable that affects the results that was not foreseen by the researcher. It may disguise what the researcher initially believed were actual associations between variables. The researcher's integrity and the integrity of his or her research requires the researcher to report any confounding factors that may have influenced the study's results (Office of Research Integrity, 2007). The researcher's responsibility is to report these factors to the best of his or her knowledge, even when the confounding factors mitigate the researcher's primary results. The reporting of confounding factors reduces *researcher bias.* The identification of confounding factors in qualitative research may be a greater issue for the researcher because of the complex nature of the observation of human interaction and difficulties associated with isolating confounding factors (Dervin & Reinhard, 2006; Oxford Reference Online, 2007).

> Confounding factors are located in the methodology or results chapter, depending on departmental norms.

Example

In this example, the researcher describes the influence of confounding factors on the researcher's study and subsequent findings.

Confounding Factors

> The factors proposed in each explanation to account for the relationship between race-ethnicity and internal school suspension can be understood as confounding factors or mediating factors. A confounding factor is defined as a third factor that is associated with both a focal independent variable and a dependent variable, and one that distorts the true relationship between the independent and the dependent variables (Fitzmaurice, 2003; Frank, 2000; Greenland & Morgenstern, 2001). The presence of confounding effects suggests that a third factor or factors explain, at least par-

tially, the observed relation between an independent variable and a dependent variable (MacKinnon, Krull, & Lockwood, 2000; Müllner, Matthews, & Altman, 2002). A mediating factor, on the other hand, refers to a third factor through which a focal independent variable affects a dependent variable (Baron & Kenny, 1986). That is, the independent variable influences the mediating factor, which, in turn, influences the dependent variable (Sobel, 1990). What makes a mediating factor conceptually different from a confounding factor is that the concept of mediating factor involves a clearly defined causal-effect relationship between an independent variable and a mediating factor, and such a relationship between a mediating factor and a dependent variable.

In this study, the term *confounding factor* is used preferably over the term *mediating factor* for two reasons. First, some of the third factors identified in the explanation approaches can be considered confounding factors but not mediating factors from a conceptual standpoint. A good example is unsafe and disorderly school environments. It is illogical to assume that student race-ethnicity, an individual (or level-1) characteristic, causes unsafe and disorderly school environment, a school level (or level-2) characteristic. As Krull and Mackinnon (2001) clarify, a variable at a lower level should not be modeled to affect a variable at a higher level in a multilevel mediating factor mechanism. (Jung, 2006, pp. 75–76)

Confounding Factors Checklist

- ☐ Identify and report confounding factors even if they mitigate the study's findings.
- ☐ Describe how the confounding factors disguised the relationships between the study's primary variables.

CONNECTION OF FINDINGS OR RESULTS TO THE LITERATURE

In the final chapter of the dissertation, the researcher examines the theoretical and empirical research that served as the foundation for the study. The researcher then presents an argument as to how the study's *findings* or *results* extend and support the theoretical constructs on which the study was based. If the study's *findings* or *results* contradict the theoretical constructs, the researcher offers a rationale for new theory. In some cases, the researcher may demonstrate how his or her findings extend established theory. The researcher applies the same process of linking findings to the empirical research that served as the inquiry tradition for the study (see *implications for future research*).

> Connection of the findings or results to the literature is located in the discussion chapter.

Connection of the Findings or Results to the Literature Checklist

- ☐ Re-state the theoretical perspectives that guided the study.
- ☐ Identify how the study's *findings* or *results* support, extend, or contradict the theoretical perspectives that guided the study.

CONSTRUCT VALIDITY

The researcher provides a description of how she or he obtained construct validity in *Chapter 3* (*methodology chapter*) under the subheading of "Research Quality." Construct validity refers to the exact measurement of constructs by tests or other procedures. In essence, construct validity assesses the degree to which the test or other procedures measure what they claim to measure. There are three types of construct validity: concurrent validity, content validity, and predictive validity (Bagozzi, Youjae, & Phillips, 1991; Heffner, 2004).

> The construct validity section is located in the methodology chapter.

Example

In this example, the researcher describes the evidence for the presence of construct validity in the study.

Construct Validity

> Capraro and Capraro (2002) found that several researchers have studied the construct validity of the MBTI, correlating the scores with findings from various personality instruments and inventories. Significant corre-

lations have been found between MBTI scores, behaviors of the constructs, and a person's self-assessment of their type (Capraro & Capraro 2002).

Carlson (1989) discussed what is called psychological validity, meaning that the test takers and those around them often agree that their results are appropriate. In fact, in many cases, people can estimate fairly closely what their results will be, after learning about the different dimensions, before actually receiving them back (Carlson1989).

Ring (1998) further discussed the validity of the MBTI, stating that research has been done since the publication of the last manual, including several more sophisticated tests on the convergent, divergent, and predictive qualities of the MBTI. There have been many exploratory and confirmatory factor analytic studies that have produced four-factor structures almost identical to the preference scoring system's (Ring, 1998). Going further, type tables have been widely used to support the MBTI's validity (Ring, 1998). Type tables are a method of looking at the sixteen types for multiple people at once (McCaulley, 1990). Because these tables can display type information for a number of individuals simultaneously, researchers and counselors have a graphical means of exploring data for groups (McCaulley, 1990). These provide evidence for construct validity by showing that a significantly higher percentage of certain types fall within an area of interest than could be expected by chance (Ring, 1998). In correlating the MBTI results with the only other instrument that measures Jungian types, there is a significant commonality of constructs that are hit on by both (Ring, 1998). There is more consistency for the EI and SN scales than TF (Ring, 1998). (L. Brown, 2006, pp. 42–43)

Construct Validity Checklist

- ☐ Describe the procedures to ascertain construct validity.
- ☐ Describe the three features of construct validity: concurrent validity, content validity, and predictive validity.

CONTEXT OF THE STUDY

The context of the study section describes the social context of the *unit of analysis* and is often found in qualitative dissertations. Miles and Huberman state:

> Most qualitative researchers believe that a person's behavior has to be understood in a specific context, and that the context cannot be ignored or "held constant." The context can be seen as immediately relevant aspects of the situation—where the person is physically, who else is involved, what the relevant aspects of the social system are in which the person appears. (1994, p. 102)

In describing the context of the study, the researcher may include rich descriptions of the characteristics of the *unit of analysis* and the cultural, organizational, and social factors that may influence the data (Evans, Leake, McMullen, & Bogaerts, 2005).

> In a traditional dissertation, the context of the study is located in the methodology chapter.

Example

In this example, the researcher describes the context in which data were gathered. The researcher describes personal involvement in this context as well as similar contexts.

Context of the Study

> Another trait of qualitative data collection and analysis is that the researcher functions as the primary instrument for data collection and analysis (Merriam, 1988). Lincoln and Guba (1985) state that in this role, the researcher responds to the context of the study, processes information, and classifies and summarizes data. In this particular research, the researcher's involvement in the educational profession as an administrator and teacher for the last fifteen years provided valuable insight into the data analysis. This insight was further sharpened, since the researcher experienced some of the changes high-stakes testing has brought to the central office culture. That stated, however, there were some disadvantages of being an insider. It is possible that principals were reluctant to discuss central office impact with a central office administrator in the district. At times, employees may have suspected some other purpose for collecting

the data. Thus, it was critical that subjectivity and rapport were considered throughout the research process. Just as viewing the researcher as the primary instrument of research has distinct advantages and challenges, qualitative research in general has strengths and weaknesses. (Champion, 2007, p. 64)

Context of the Study Checklist

- ☐ Fully identify and describe relevant contextual factors.
- ☐ Fully describe the characteristics of the unit of analysis.
- ☐ Describe aspects of the context that contribute to understanding participant behavior.

D

DATA ANALYSIS (see Analysis [Qualitative] and Analysis [Quantitative])

DATA COLLECTION

The data collection section describes the methods, procedures, and characteristics of the sample or unit of analysis. The data collection methods indicate the type of inquiry (quantitative, qualitative, mixed methods) the researcher will use, as well as the type of data the researcher will collect. The researcher carefully describes in rich detail the definitions of the terms and how she or he will use them in the study. The researcher states the time, location, and length of data collection activities (Council of the American Educational Research Association, 2006). The researcher avoids jargon and rote text descriptions; instead, the researcher focuses on how he or she collected data and the means used to collect data. The researcher also describes procedures used to collect data, how data collection occurred, who collected data, where data were collected, and any confounding issues that affected data collection. The researcher concludes the data collection section by describing how each method is relevant to the *research design* and *research questions* or *hypotheses* (Office of Behavioral and Social Sciences Research, 2001).

> The data collection section is located in the methodology chapter.

Example

In this example, the researcher provides a detailed description of data collection methods. The researcher indicates the type of data collected and the source of data.

Data Collection Methods

The data collection methods included background information on the school. This background information provided an overview of the environment in which learning takes place, including the physical plant, school vision, school climate (such as safety and discipline), the curricula, teaching strategies, and educational materials.

The participants were presented with a survey. The survey was designed as a two-sided questionnaire. The first side of the questionnaire focused on demographic characteristics, which are consistently found to impact educational decisions. The questionnaire was designed to provide a descriptive profile of the parent group. The questionnaire also included items related to child characteristics such as interests, learning preferences, disability or gifted, and particular aptitudes. The child's age and grade level and whether parents have more than one child in the school were a part of the research design.

The survey questionnaire contained items relating to reasons for choosing a school. The questionnaire included items on academic emphasis, test scores, values, class size, individualized instruction, learning environment, discipline, safety, racial and ethnic diversity, convenience, proximity, teaching strategies, curriculum, and educational resources and materials. . . .

Additional questions addressed the sources of information that parents used to determine their choice of schools. . . . The questionnaires were designed with open-ended questions and a space for parents to add additional comments. An additional data source was semi-structured interviews. . . . The self-report close-ended survey questions were supplemented with semi-structured interviews for more in-depth analysis. This study synthesized survey data with parent interviews. (Parker, 2007, pp. 89–91)

Data Collection Checklist

- ☐ Identify and describe all data collection methods.
- ☐ Describe the procedures used to collect data.
- ☐ Describe confounding issues related to data collection.
- ☐ Describe how data collection methods are related to the *research design*, *research questions*, and *hypotheses*.

DATA SOURCES (also Sources of Evidence)

The researcher describes his or her data sources in this section. Some refer to data sources as *sources of evidence.* The researcher provides rich descriptions of the *units of analysis* or sample when describing data sources. The researcher also describes the rationale for participant inclusion into the *units of analysis* as well as any other data source. The researcher informs the reader how the data collected address the *research questions* or *hypotheses.* Data sources often include any or all of the following (Council of the American Educational Research Association, 2006):

- Artifacts
- Audio- or video-recordings
- Categorical demographic information
- Documents such as agenda, blogs, data bases, wikis, e-mails, minutes, newspapers, and reports
- Observations
- Standardized instruments
- Structured interview protocols
- Unstructured or semi-structured interviews

> The data sources are located in the methodology chapter.

Example

In the following example, the researcher identifies data sources and then elaborates on each data source.

Data Sources

Multiple secondary data sources were utilized for the purpose of the study. The sources were as follows: results of the evaluation of Bowling Green State University (BGSU) Assessment of Technology Competency (ATC); the ATC Retake Survey results; the Ohio Department of Education (ODE) Similar District computation report from fiscal year 2003–2004; and the Ohio SchoolNet (OSN) Biennial Education Technology Assessment

(BETA) district-level teacher survey from the biennial academic year 2003–2005. (Goedde, 2006, p. 47)

Data Sources Checklist

- ☐ Describe each data source.
- ☐ Link each data source to the *research questions* or *hypotheses.*
- ☐ Provide a rationale for inclusion into the *unit of analysis* or *sample.*

DEDICATION

A dedication page is found in most dissertations. The dedication is a symbol of the researcher's respect and admiration for persons either living or deceased. It may refer to the researcher's spiritual tradition, organizations, or symbols, and the role they played in his or her life. The length of the dedication ranges from a simple sentence to a paragraph.

> The dedication is located prior to acknowledgment and after the copyright and approval pages.

Example

The dedication may be a one-sentence dedication, or, as in this case, the dedication may reference several people who played instrumental roles in the researcher's life.

Dedication

The completion of this work would never have been possible without three very important people, and it is to them that I dedicate this work.

My mother, Margaret Younger, and her never-ending support made all of this possible. She has believed in me since I began this endeavor and has been my strongest advocate in making this dream of mine a reality.

My father, J. E. Younger, whose calm strength I admire more that I can say, has inspired me with his wisdom, his courage, and his enduring sense of humor. How fortunate our family is to have him in our lives.

> My amazing son, Kristofer Wainwright Berry, really is the *wind beneath my wings*. He has always supported my endeavors to advance my education, even when it meant sacrificing our time together. Beyond all else, he is by far the greatest joy in my life, my most precious blessing, and the accomplishment of which I am most proud. (Russell Berry, 2004, p. v)

Dedication Checklist

- ☐ The dedication references someone who is admired by the researcher.
- ☐ The dedication is brief, poignant, and meaningful.

DEFINITION OF TERMS (also Key Terms)

The definition of terms or *key terms* section identifies those terms the researcher considers essential to report his or her study. The terms identified are precisely defined to communicate the meaning that the researcher used in applying the term to the research. The researcher supports the definition of the term with appropriate citations. The term is then consistently applied throughout the dissertation.

> The definition of terms section is located in the introductory chapter.

Example

In this example, the researcher lists the definition of terms used in the study. In some cases, the researcher provides citations to support the definition of the key term.

Definition of Key Terms

1. *Academic achievement.* Meeting grade-level standards.
2. *At-risk.* A student who is struggling to meet grade-level standards and is a candidate for retention.
3. *Beliefs.* Are based on experiences and knowledge, which individuals assume to be true.
4. *Cronbach's Alpha* "... determine the degree to which all the items are measuring the same construct" (Cronk, 1999, p. 102).

5. *Construct validity.* "The degree to which an instrument measures an intended hypothetical psychology construct or nonobservable trait" (Fraenkel & Wallen, 2003, p. G-2).
6. *Descriptive statistics.* Descriptive statistics are used to describe a large amount of data using a few indices (Fraenkel & Wallen, 2003; Trochim, 2002).
7. *Discriminant analysis.* "To predict membership in a particular group for new or future subjects from the same population" (Mertler & Vannatta, 2006, p. 282).
8. *Eigenvalue.* "The amount of variance of the variables accounted for by a factor" (Green & Salkind, 2003, p. 301).
9. *Factor analysis.* "Technique used to identify factors that statistically explain the variation and covariation among measures" (Green & Salkind, 2003, p. 296).
10. *Grade retention.* The practice of retaining a student in the current grade due to the student's failure to master required academic standards.
11. *Graded school.* The organization of students by grades such as first, second, third, and so forth. (Hayes III, 2007, pp. 7–8)

Definition of Terms Checklist

- ☐ Precisely define each term to identify the way it is used in the dissertation.
- ☐ Support each definition with appropriate, substantive citations (where appropriate, preferably from seminal research).
- ☐ Define only terms essential to the study.

DELIMITATIONS

The researcher uses the term *delimitations* to indicate how she or he narrowed the study to focus on specific aspects. According to Creswell (2002), the researcher indicates how she or he chose to narrow the specific focus of the study by identifying a precise type of research methodology, participant characteristic, context or research site, or phenomenon studied during the research.

> Delimitations are located in the introductory chapter.

Example

Delimitations

The design of this study, of necessity, sets boundaries to the scope of this research. Some of the restrictions were:

1. The entire population of union directors was not sampled and directors from colleges not were included. This is particularly worth noting when considering that the majority of member schools in ACUI (and American higher education institutions) have a student population of 5000 or less.

2. The survey data was gathered only from incumbent executive directors. No information was sought from those who hire and supervise the directors. While a survey of the supervisors was beyond the scope of this study, the researcher recognizes the potential value of supervisors' opinions in helping to define the skills and knowledge of a competent union director.

3. Only directors of universities in the United States were included in this study. No attempt was made to survey directors of college unions in other nations. (Moore Morton, 1999, p. 13)

Delimitations Checklist

- ☐ Describe how the delimitation narrows the scope of the study.
- ☐ Describe how the delimitation identifies participants, the research methodology, the site, or the phenomenon.

DEMOGRAPHIC CHARACTERISTICS

The researcher uses the demographic characteristics section to describe the unit of analysis or sample for the study. The researcher's description includes rich detail of the central or social descriptors of the participants or sample in the study. Examples of descriptors most notably found in qualitative research designs include information about participants including age, gender, level of education, religion, and ethnicity. The rich descriptions will include placing demographic information about participants in specific social and cultural contexts.

In quantitative studies, demographic characteristics may be referred to as *demographic variables*. If the researcher uses demographic variables, she or he will report any statistically significant differences among the variables. She or he will reference appropriate tables within the dissertation. The tables follow the appropriate style set by the researcher's graduate school and department.

> Demographic characteristics or demographic variables are located in the methodology chapter.

Example

The following is a straightforward example of presenting demographic data. Researchers may also present demographic data in a narrative format.

Demographic Characteristics/Demographic Variables

Demographic information for the current sample is presented in Table 1. There were 40 (13.5%) males and 256 (86.5%) females that composed the sample. Racially/ethnically the participants were mostly Caucasian (267 or 90.2%). The remaining 9.8% included 20 (6.8%) African American, six (2.0%) Hispanic, five (1.0%) Other, and zero (0%) Asian individuals.

With respect to age, there were 44 individuals (14.9%) aged 21 to 30, 79 individuals (26.7%) aged 31 to 40, 77 individuals (26.0%) aged 41 to 50, 87 individuals (29.4%) aged 51 to 60, and nine individuals (3.0%) over the age of 60. Years of teaching experience, and age-related demographics, is reported as follows: 11 (3.7%) had zero to one year of teaching experience, 54 (18.2%) had two to five years of teaching experience, 57 (19.3%) had six to 10 years of teaching experience, 83 (28.0%) had 11 to 20 years of teaching experience, and 91 (30.7%) had more than 20 years of teaching experience.

Participants identified themselves in reference to marital status in the following manner: 44 (14.9%) single, 209 (70.6%) married, 16 (5.4%) significant other but unmarried, 26 (8.8%) separated/divorced, and one (0.3%) widowed. In terms of number of children, 99 (33.4%) participants reported having no children, 55 (18.6%) participants reported having children not residing with them, and 142 (48.0%) participants reported having children who do reside with them.

> In terms of miles of commute, most participants lived near their schools. Ninety one individuals (30.7%) reported commuting zero to five miles, 67 (22.6%) reported traveling six to 10 miles, 73 (24.7%) commuted 11 to 20 miles, 27 (9.1%) reported traveling 21 to 30 miles, and 38 (12.8%) reported commuting greater than 30 miles. (Senholzi, 2005, p. 44)

Demographic Variables/Characteristics Checklist

- ☐ Describe each demographic variable or characteristic.
- ☐ Identify each demographic variable or characteristic as a descriptive of the unit of analysis or sample.
- ☐ Report statistically significant differences of demographic variables in appropriate tables.

DEPENDENT VARIABLES

In quantitative research, the researcher operationally defines the dependent variables prior to their measurement (usually in the dissertation proposal stage). The value of the dependent variable depends on the influence of the independent variable. In a study to determine if there is a relationship between teacher age and their students' achievement, the teacher's age is the supposed cause (independent variable) and the students' achievement is the effect (dependent variable). The researcher describes the effect of the *independent variables* in the study on the dependent variables (Babbie, 2004). The effect of the *independent variable* on the dependent variable is measured and the effect is reported in the researcher's dissertation. The researcher remembers to describe any cause and effect relationship between the *variables.*

> Dependent variables are located in the methodology chapter or with results and findings.

Example 1

In the first example, the researcher identifies the dependent variables used in the study. In the second example, the research identifies and describes the dependent variables used in the study.

Dependent Variables

The dependent variables identified in this study were knowledge and skills, instructional techniques and practices, confidence in teaching abilities, and relationships with children and their families. (Duncan, 2008, p. 12)

Example 2

The dependent variables used in this study were high school students' academic achievement, engagement, attendance, and attitude toward school. Student academic achievement was represented by the average of students' most recent percentage grades in science, social studies, English language arts, and mathematics. Student engagement was a self-reported measure of the amount of time that students spend involved in school-related activities. Attendance was drawn from answers to survey questions, reported directly by the student. Attendance was expressed as a percent and reflected the number of class periods absent from school during the last full semester attended by the student. Student attitude scores were drawn from the results of the School Attitude Assessment Survey-Revised (2002). (Mombourquette, 2007, p. 41)

Dependent Variables Checklist

- ☐ Describe each dependent variable.
- ☐ Operationally define each dependent variable.
- ☐ Describe the differences in dependent variables and illustrate them in appropriate tables.

DESCRIPTION (OF PARTICIPANT GROUPS) (see Demographic Characteristics)

DESCRIPTIVE DATA

Descriptive data provide descriptions of the researcher's immersion in the research setting, reflective insights from collected data, depth and breadth of the participants' experiences, and the inferences generated by the descriptive data. Data is a plural term. Remember to speak and write "data were"; note the next sentence as an example. Descriptive data were also reported in numeric format in quantitative studies to describe the sample or the population from which the sample was drawn (Holosko, 2001). The researcher reports descriptive data in the results section based on the researcher's application of descriptive statistics in data analysis.

> The descriptive data are located in the methodology chapter or the results chapter.

Example 1

Descriptive Data

The respondents' demographic data were processed and analyzed using descriptive statistics. Frequency of response percentages were converted to percentages and used to analyze the importance of specific law topics and the utilization of various methods and means of continuing education opportunities. Analysis also included a comparison of domain response percentage means and mean ranks thereof. Results from Part I of the survey, Demographic Information, were utilized to provide descriptive data regarding the respondents. Data identifying the respondents as superintendents, principals, and education law attorneys, as well as subcategories of principals (i.e., elementary school, middle school, high school), were utilized for Part I survey data analysis.

From Part II of the survey, Important Areas of School Law for Principals, the results were utilized to provide comparative analyses of responses from the three main respondent groups (superintendents, principals, education law attorneys), and of the three principal subgroups (elementary, middle school, high school), specific to both the individual school law knowledge areas as well as the six overall school law domains. For school law knowledge essential to public school principals, an additional comparative analysis of responses was conducted of specific areas and domains based on principal and superintendent district enrollment size subgroups. (Magone, 2007, pp. 43–44)

Example 2

Descriptive Data

Data obtained corresponded with the independent variables of transformational leadership, institution type, respondent sex, age, and years of experience. In addition, the dependent variable of state match status and related monetary amounts was also garnered.

Transformational leadership was operationalized in both nominal and ordinal scales. Respondents either scored as low transformational leaders (mean score of 0.0 to 2.0) or high transformational leaders (2.1 to 4.0). In addition, total mean score was calculated for each respondent. All 87 participants (100%) identified themselves to be highly transformational leaders, as their mean score was 3.35.

Type of land-grant institution was operationalized categorically (1862 or 1890). Responses were received from 63 administrators (N = 87, 72.4%) of sixteen 1862 cooperative extension programs (out of a total of 17, 94.1%). Responses were also received from 24 administrators (N = 87, 27.6%) of fifteen 1890 cooperative extension programs (out of a total of 18, 83.3%). Thirty-one (31) of 35 institutions are reflected in the data, or 88.6%.

Sex of the 1862 and 1890 extension administrator was another categorical predictor variable. Of the 87 participants, there were 54 males (62.1%) and 33 females (37.9%) who responded to the survey questionnaire.

Age of the 1862 and 1890 extension administrator was categorized on the questionnaire by five-year intervals. Respondents could select from 12 categories of age ranges, commencing with the 25–29 year interval and ending with the 80–84 year interval. There were 83 valid cases for which data could be analyzed. The age range with the highest frequency of administrators was 50–54 years (32.2%).

Years of experience were entered as ratio level data. There were 80 valid cases from which data could be analyzed. The average years of experience of the participant in his or her respective current position were 10.1. (Ali, 2005, pp. 88–90)

Descriptive Data Checklist

- ☐ Describe descriptive data in full detail to provide a deep and broad understanding of the participant.
- ☐ The descriptive data, if numerical or statistical, accurately describes the sample or population from which the participant was drawn.
- ☐ Remember that data is a plural term.

DESCRIPTIVE STATISTICS

The researcher uses descriptive statistics to provide the reader with a description of the sample or population from which his or her sample was drawn. Descriptive statistics provide measures of central tendency and summaries in numerical form. The researcher may report the mean, median, and mode of the study sample or population. The researcher also describes the distribution of data through various measures: variance, standard deviation, or interquartile ranges (Kessler, 2008).

Example

In this example, the researcher provides the descriptive statistics of the study's dependent variables. The researcher provides the reader with accurate statistical data.

> ***Descriptive Statistics of the Dependent Variables***
>
> The dependent variables of interest in this study were the statewide LEA measurements of AYP attainment in reading and AYP math. Of the 149 Mississippi LEAs, 59.1% did not attain AYP in reading. Additionally, 48.3% of Mississippi LEAs did not attain AYP in math. These statistics reveal the critical need for a predictive diagnostic model for AYP in reading and math so that proactive measures such as remedial academic programs, intensive professional development workshops, or the adoption of appropriate comprehensive school reform models can be implemented to increase the likelihood that LEAs will meet federal standards. The descriptive statistics for these variables are presented in Tables 1 and 2. (Moore, 2006, p. 47)

Descriptive Statistics Checklist

- ☐ Describe descriptive statistics in full detail with reference to appropriate tables.
- ☐ The descriptive statistics show measures of central tendency as well as the distribution of the data.
- ☐ Report only relevant descriptive statistics.

DESIGN OF THE STUDY (see Research Design)

DIRECTION FOR FUTURE RESEARCH (see Future Research)

DISCUSSION (also Chapter 5)

The *discussion* section of the dissertation affords the researcher the opportunity to provide the reader with speculative opinions, interpretation, and implications of the study's *findings* and *results* for research or praxis. The discussion does not repeat the *findings* or *results*. The discussion, however, allows the researcher to describe how his or her study contributes to the continuity of the line inquiry. In presenting the discussion, the researcher may describe the study's strengths and weaknesses as they contributed to or detracted from the study's outcomes (The Writing Centre, 2006). Wording is important in the discussion section. The researcher uses words or phrases such as *may, appear to, contributes in part,* and *might.* The researcher provides a rationale for the outcome linking to the study's theoretical perspectives or a new theory that helps to better explain the study's findings.

The discussion is located in the discussion chapter (usually Chapter 5).

Example

In the following example, the researcher added a discussion section after each finding.

Discussion

In general, most schools that educate limited English proficient (LEP) students provide some type of special assistance that is conceptualized in this study as methods that facilitate the involvement of language minority parents at the school. Most of the school characteristics examined in this chapter were related to facilitation efforts, as evidenced in the correlation analyses. However, the regression analyses, in which many characteristics were controlled simultaneously, showed that some of these relationships were indirect, some were spurious, and some were direct but conditioned by other factors.

As expected, facilitation was greater in schools with larger percentages of LEP students. However, this positive relationship disappeared once other factors, specifically percent Latino and Asian teachers and the number of ESL/bilingual teachers and aides employed by a school, were controlled. Therefore, the relationship between the percentage of LEP students in a school and facilitation of the involvement of LM/LEP families appears to be indirect, primarily through the characteristics of the teachers and aides a school employs. Specifically, when a larger percentage of a school's student population is LEP, it hires more ESL/bilingual teachers and/or aides to address LEP students' language and educational needs. In turn, schools with more ESL/bilingual teachers and aides offer more types of assistance to LM/LEP families that may facilitate these families' involvement. (Mulligan, 2005, p. 243)

Discussion Checklist

- ☐ The discussion is the researcher's interpretation for the reasons why the study produced its outcomes.
- ☐ The discussion presents implications for future research and praxis.
- ☐ The discussion identifies and describes new theoretical perspectives that help to explain the *findings* and *results.*
- ☐ The discussion does not repeat the *findings* and *results* of the study.

DISSERTATION OUTLINE (see Organization of the Study)

DOCUMENTS

Documents are a data source in empirical research. The researcher describes the documents and data the researcher expects to collect from the documents. She or he relates these data to the *research questions* or *hypotheses.* The researcher provides citations for the documents in the reference section. The researcher may also provide copies of relevant documents (depending on length) in an *appendix.* If the researcher is using a qualitative research design, she or he indicates how the relevant documents contribute to the triangulation of data. In some cases, the researcher may embed a digital picture into the document and place it in an *appendix*. If the researcher used a database as the primary source of data for the study, she or he describes the source, provides a rationale for analyzing the database, and links his or her inquiry to relevant inferential statistical analysis. An executive summary of the database source may be placed in an *appendix*.

The documents are located in the methodology chapter.

Example

In this example, the researcher identifies the documents that are the source of data for the researcher's study.

Document Collection

> Documents collected from each of the school sites included office memos, newsletters, accreditation reports, district-office communications, and principals' reports, as well as copies of each site's educational profile, parent/student handbooks, and registration procedures. Documents collected at each school helped provide a fuller understanding of the school's climate and overall goals. Analysis of documents allowed for triangulation of data from interviews and observations. (Barringer, 2006, p. 55)

Documents Checklist

- ☐ Demonstrate how the relevant documents assist in triangulating data, especially if using a qualitative research design.
- ☐ Provide a rationale for using a database document as the source of data for statistical analysis.
- ☐ Describe only relevant documents in the dissertation.
- ☐ Place copies of relevant documents, embedded digitalized pictures of relevant documents, or executive summaries of documents in appropriate *appendices*.

E

EMERGENT DESIGN

Emergent design occurs when the researcher uses a form of naturalistic inquiry with the understanding that the research design evolves as she or he collects data (Patton, 2002). The researcher describes how the collected data necessitated alterations in the original research design. The researcher's defense of an emergent design is based on rigorous planning in the original research plan and an openness to insights gained from collected data to open new lines of inquiry. The researcher describes his or her rationale in presenting an argument for an emergent design.

The emergent design is located in the methodology chapter.

Example

The researcher explains emergent design as a component of qualitative research and explains its place in the research design.

Emergent Design

> Given the flexible and emergent design of qualitative research, the researcher recorded design decisions in a journal as a strategy to further monitor and evaluate researcher subjectivity. Judgments about data validity, data management techniques, codes, categories and decision rules were recorded throughout the research process. This chapter summarized the researcher's assumptions and the qualitative methods used in the study. The transcribed interviews with the twenty-five African American women participants became the data for the study. The analysis of the interviews

revealed salient themes related to the substance abuse histories, treatment experiences and needs of this sample of women. The themes that emerged from the analysis of the interviews are presented in the following section on study findings. (Hill, 2005, p. 82)

Emergent Design Checklist

- ☐ Provide a rationale for altering the original research design.
- ☐ Describe how an emergent design will yield new theory and important outcomes that were not considered when the research was initiated.
- ☐ Plan in the study's research design for the possibility of an emergent design.

EMPIRICAL RESEARCH

The researcher often refers to empirical research during the literature review. The researcher examines only research where collected data are based on observations or measurement of observed phenomenon (Trochim, 2001). The researcher describes the plan for selection of relevant empirical research. In doing so, she or he seeks to identify common themes, gaps, patterns, and outcomes relevant to the researcher's line of inquiry (Calabrese, 2006). The researcher (1) begins with a description of the relevant empirical research, (2) provides criteria for inclusion and exclusion, (3) includes questions that guide the search for relevant empirical research, and (4) adds a set of findings discovered in the review. The researcher uses these findings to outline the presentation of relevant empirical research.

> The empirical research is located in the literature review chapter.

Example

The researcher in the example presents a summary of the relevant empirical research.

Empirical Research

The empirical evidence suggests that cooperative education does contribute to clarification of career goals, self-confidence, awareness of inter-

> personal relationships, and increased motivation. General impressions are almost always positive; however, Stern et al. (1990) suggested that while research does find that students enrolled in cooperative education are relatively satisfied with school, there is not consistent evidence that they learn more, become more productive, or find better jobs. Stern and his associates maintained that methodological problems with the evaluations may mask stronger positive outcomes from cooperative education participation. They concluded that even though positive economic outcomes are not shown, there is some indication that students who participate in cooperative education are finding higher quality jobs than high school students find on their own. This group of researchers argued that cooperative education placements provide students with positions of greater responsibility, better supervision, mentoring, and more opportunities to learn complex skills. Using data from one western state, Stevens (1993) also found that students with cooperative education job placements who remained with the same employer after leaving school experienced higher earnings than students not enrolled in cooperative education who also remained with the same employers. (Moore, 1997, p. 24)

Empirical Research Checklist

- ☐ Identify the gaps, themes, patterns, or common findings in the relevant empirical research.
- ☐ Provide a description of the criteria used to select relevant empirical research.
- ☐ Present the analysis of the relevant empirical research in a logical format.

EPILOGUE

Some researchers provide an epilogue as a summary chapter of the dissertation. An epilogue is often found more frequently in lengthy qualitative research dissertations where there is a sizeable amount of rich descriptive data presented in narrative format. The researcher summarizes the study's story in the epilogue. The epilogue is the last chapter in the qualitative, research-driven dissertation.

> The epilogue is the last chapter in the dissertation.

Example

In this example, the researcher uses the epilogue to provide the reader with the researcher's personal reflection.

Epilogue

> "I [have] learned that my gift as a teacher is the ability to dance with my students, to co-create with them a context in which all of us teach and learn" (Palmer, 1998, p. 72). In light of what this research has discovered, I think back now to the experiences I have had as a wilderness guide and the experiences I have had as a teacher in the classroom. Even though many of my guided clients expressed their appreciation of providing a meaningful learning experience, interestingly, I now think that not all of my students from the classroom setting failed to get a meaningful learning experience by studying the facts of introductory biology. I am sure that some students must have seen my course as a risk and felt the awkwardness of experiencing . . . something new. Were they fractionally sublimated? I may make a case that some were. In my biology class, it did not matter whether you were the star football player for the high school or the grand thespian of the drama department to learn the course's material. I do not think that any of my students gained an advantage in my class if they came from a wealthy family or a not so wealthy family. In other words, the social facades that the students may have been carrying around probably did not help them learn biology. But I do think some recognized and accepted their weaknesses and strengths in learning the material, and by reforming through some degree of diligent studying, they realized their potentials by achieving success in the class. Occasionally, but not often, I have received letters from former students expressing gratitude for what they learned in my class and some of the letters let me know that they are practicing medicine or doing work in the biological sciences now. (Taniguchi, 2004, p. 122)

Epilogue Checklist

- ☐ As the last chapter, the epilogue summarizes the dissertation.
- ☐ Since the epilogue is usually found in qualitative dissertations, it brings closure to the story told by the qualitative study.

ETHICAL CONSIDERATIONS

The researcher describes ethical considerations encountered during the research. In most cases, ethical considerations safeguarding the rights of the participants are presented as a precursor to the research and as part of the researcher's Institutional Review Board (IRB). There are times when ethical considerations arise during the conduct of the research. The researcher acknowledges the ethical considerations and describes them as they relate to confidentiality, informed consent, anonymity, debriefing, and the resolution to those issues (Babbie, 2004). In every case, the researcher will provide the rationale of his or her efforts and precautions to protect research participants.

> Ethical considerations are located in the methodology or the discussion chapter.

Example

In this example, the researcher describes the precautions taken to protect the participants.

Ethical Considerations

> The participants who volunteered for this study allowed me to enter into their lives for a brief period of time. It was important to assign anonymity to the participants so that they were able to maintain their own lives without any embarrassment or apprehension. In this research investigation, I portrayed each participant as accurately as possible and in an ethically responsible manner while conforming to research standards and the guidelines of this study. I distributed and retrieved signed assent forms from the participants and consent forms from the parents of the participants. The participants reviewed their transcribed interviews for accuracy and clarity. All data, including audiotapes, written transcripts, and field notes, were secured in my home office to provide security and confidentiality. The participants benefited from this study by meeting and associating with young women who were not in their usual clique. They went beyond their social comfort zones and shared their lives with unknown peers. When the participants and I would meet in my room during lunchtime to review the transcriptions, they

> were initially very timid. As the participants became more familiar with one another from meetings and discussions together, a bond began to form where the participants would talk and laugh among themselves. It appeared they began to enjoy the camaraderie of our shared journey. If my transcribing was taking too long in between meetings, one of the participants would surely remind me of the delay in our meetings. Another participant benefit from this study was a ticket to a nearby educational entertainment attraction. I provided each participant with a ticket as a thank you for sharing her stories. (Crim, 2006, pp. 56–57)

Ethical Considerations Checklist

- ☐ Provide a description of the safeguards used to protect participants in the study.
- ☐ Describe ethical issues that arose during the conduct of the research.
- ☐ Describe the resolution of ethical issues that arose during the conduct of the research.
- ☐ Describe how informed consent was gained—use description if protected populations were involved in the study.
- ☐ Describe how the participants' anonymity or confidentiality was protected.

EXTERNAL VALIDITY

The external validity of the researcher's study describes how the investigator's research is generalizable to a larger population outside those in the study. The external validity of the study is linked to the internal validity of the study. The internal validity has to be ensured before any case can be made for external validity (Guba & Lincoln, 1981). The researcher often describes how the research design may mitigate the study's external validity in the limitations section. In quantitative studies, the researcher operates from a priori stipulations that control sample size, populations, and control and test groups. In qualitative studies, Merriam (2001) suggests that the researcher use rich, thick descriptions, comparisons with similar groups or populations, and a design that includes multiple sites.

> External validity is located in the methodology chapter.

Example

In this example, the researcher acknowledges the potential threat to external validity, then addresses the challenge to external validity.

External Validity

> One important and potentially problematic aspect of this sample in terms of its external validity was that it predominantly consisted of female participants (98% of the participants were female). Although using a predominantly female sample may have created some problems because of previous findings in the justice literature that show some differences between male and female respondents, I do not believe that this created major problems. First, the composition of the sample was not because of any particular characteristic of the hospital, but a characteristic of nursing practice in Turkey (to some extent even in the United States). Second, and perhaps more importantly, Kahn, Nelson and Gaeddert (1980) suggested that sex differences in allocations situations are more likely to occur when situational demands are weak. Given that organizational contexts are strong situations (Davis-Blake & Pfeffer, 1989), the authors argue that sex differences in the past research have been exaggerated. Thus, considering the potential advantages of conducting a field study, I do not expect the sample's nature to be a limitation for the study. (Gogus, 2005, pp. 49–50)

External Validity Checklist

- ☐ Provide a description that links internal validity to external validity.
- ☐ Provide a rationale of how the findings and results are generalized.
- ☐ Describe how the findings and results in the study can be expected to occur under the same circumstances to similar populations outside the study.

F

FEEDBACK AND PARTICIPANTS

Participant feedback is essential to verify data or findings and results. It is also an ethical obligation on the researcher's part to provide feedback to the participant as quickly as possible after the participant's engagement in the research. The researcher describes how she or he provided feedback to the study's participants. Participant feedback may be an important consideration in many research designs; it is an important consideration in qualitative research as a means of member checking (Merriam, 2001). The researcher describes the protocols used for participant feedback and how she or he provides feedback to the study's participants. In some instances, providing feedback to participants is an Institutional Review Board (IRB) requirement. Participant feedback is an important part of member checking in qualitative studies. The researcher, depending on the type of research design used in the study, will use feedback to share the findings of the study with participants.

> Feedback to participants is located in the methodology chapter.

Example

In this example, the researcher explains how participant feedback occurred in a qualitative study.

Feedback to Participants (Participant Feedback)

> In line with this exploratory approach, the interviewer introduced the general topics and then followed up in response to the informants'

responses. The established protocol was used as a framework but modified and extended to attend to the rising themes within the study as well as to the particular concerns and direction of the informant as appropriate (Merriam, 1998). At the conclusion of the interview, the primary investigator performed an early member check by reviewing the main points of the dialogue and requesting participant feedback (Merriam). These interviews were audio taped and transcribed. (Brasfield, 2007, pp. 36–37)

Feedback Checklist

- ☐ Feedback, in some instances, is an IRB requirement; check with your institution's IRB to determine if participants are required to receive and review information regarding their participation and the study's results.
- ☐ Describe the protocols used for participant feedback.
- ☐ Describe participant response to the feedback if essential to verifying data or findings.
- ☐ Indicate how participant feedback was part of member checking.

FIELD NOTES

Field notes are the collection of the researcher's journal, reflections, observations, feelings, anecdotal comments, drawings or sketches of the research environment or artifacts, and other notations made by the researcher related to the collection of data at the research site. The researcher identifies the written or electronically recorded field notes as a data source when writing the findings and results and discussion chapters. The researcher describes how field notes were used to enhance the collection and interpretation of data. A sample of pertinent field notes can be included in the appendix to present the detail to which the researcher maintained field notes and to also highlight data pertinent to support the study's conclusions (Merriam, 2001).

> The field notes, or representative samples of field notes, are located in the appendices of the dissertation.

Example

In this example, the researcher describes the use of field notes in the conduct of the study.

Field Notes

In addition to taped interviews, the researcher wrote field notes while conducting the interviews and completed a contact summary sheet within 24 hours of each interview. Maintaining the field notes allowed the researcher to capture nuances of meaning conveyed through the participants' body language, vocal inflections, and facial expressions. The field contact summary sheet enabled the researcher to identify the main concepts, themes, issues, and questions that were raised in each interview. (Vanhook-Morrissey, 2003, p. 60)

Example

In this example, the researcher placed a sample of the field notes in the appendix.

Field Notes

Appendix E: An example of field notes: One ward / One participant
Attendance Summary of Field Notes Codes

From 8 am to 4 pm of Monday the nineteenth of December to Friday the twenty-third of December 2003, I conducted participant observation in the Male Surgical Ward. Everyday I arrived at this ward at 7:30. There were four nurses operating on morning shift and each of them started nursing practice. The process of learning happened in each period while working as follows:

One nurse checked readiness and counted quantity of the important medical tools/equipment of ward. Then, readiness and quantity of each type would be confirmed to night shift's nurses. Another nurse checked the vital signs and neuro signs of patients with severe conditions in the ward and discussed changing symptoms with night shift's nurses. Another nurse checked types and quantity of fluid/blood provided to each patient in the ward.

> In-charge nurse and other nurses in the morning team and the Head ward began handing over between night shift and morning shift. The in-charge nurse of night shift described injured and changed conditions, treatment/surgery plans, including assessment of each patient in the ward, one more time. (Nokdee, 2007, p. 188)

Field Notes Checklist

- ☐ Describe the types of field notes taken and used as a data source in the methodology chapter.
- ☐ Field notes are indicated as a data source and linked to data triangulation.
- ☐ Place field notes in the appendices. They are pertinent to supporting the study's conclusions.
- ☐ Place field notes that are comprehensive, detailed, and provide appropriate annotation in the appendices.
- ☐ Include in the field notes a description of the site, date, and time the field notes were recorded.
- ☐ Use the field notes as a tool to help with tracking other information collected at the site.

FINDINGS (also Results)

The findings header is associated with findings, analysis, and conclusions. See *analysis* and *conclusion* for definitions of those terms. The researcher presents findings based on rigorously analyzed data in the findings and results chapter. The findings are often interspersed with discussion in many dissertations. The findings are grounded and supported by evidence amassed by the researcher. The researcher inductively derives findings from data and data analysis. The researcher uses tables. They are directly linked to the research questions and hypotheses. The abstract is an appropriate place to list findings devoid of the discussion narrative.

> The findings are located in the abstract and results chapter.

Example 1

In this example, the researcher's findings are straightforward, derived directly from data, free of speculation, and are succinctly placed in the abstract.

Findings

The analysis revealed the following findings: (a) that there was no significant difference in the participant's use of discussion boards and virtual café based on age and gender, (b) that there was no significant difference in social communication based on age and gender, (c) that there was no significant difference among communication tools that would increase social communication, (d) online group discussion forums were not used more for social communications than other discussion boards and the virtual café, and (e) the pre and post questionnaires revealed that there was a positive increase in the following responses: online education is an excellent medium for social interaction, respondent's comfort level from pre to post questionnaire that they felt comfortable conversing in the online environment, and that respondents strongly agreed that online education was an excellent way for them to learn. (Carpenter, 2006, abstract).

Example 2

In this example, the researcher used qualitative methods and presents a finding using descriptive text. The researcher uses tables to clarify data. I truncated the finding to economize on space while maintaining the integrity of the finding.

Findings

Lincoln Elementary School is a Cohesive Group of Educators
Who Seek to Help Students Reach Their Potential

Lincoln Elementary School is a cohesive group of educators who seek to help students reach their potential. There was evidence that the participants' highpoint positive core teaching experiences evolved from expecting the best of their students. Data collected from the discovery and dream phases recalling highpoint positive core teaching experiences and the conditions surrounding these experiences revealed that the AI Learning Team process created a heightened awareness of the participants' desire for students to be successful and reach their potential. See Tables 4.1 and 4.2 below for participants' quotations as they relate to the first finding. Through discussions of sharing best-teaching experiences, participants identified exemplary teaching practices when students reached high points

> of success. They spoke of the importance of students being successful with a positive school experience. Participants believed creating an exciting learning environment impacted student achievement. Jake believed students were more successful when they enjoyed their experiences. Nicole shared: "I have been teaching reading to 5th graders for eight years. It is exciting to see when my struggling readers make the connections and all of a sudden something clicks and everything is falling into place. They pick up a book without pictures and begin to understand. It is just fantastic. I love what I do. I want the kids to love their experience in my classroom, but just love learning. It never stops. It is something that continues and goes on forever and forever." (Glasgow, 2008, p. 77)

Findings Checklist

- ☐ Each finding is a logical conclusion of the study and is supported by data.
- ☐ Each finding is free of interpretation and speculation.

FURTHER INQUIRY (see Future Research)

FURTHER STUDY NEEDED (see Future Research)

FUTURE RESEARCH (also Direction for Future Research)

The researcher's study provides answers to the study's research questions and hypotheses. During the course of the study, the researcher is also open to new information that raises new unanswered questions. In the future research section the researcher (1) identifies new lines of inquiry; (2) describes how these new lines of inquiry will add to the continuity between past, present, and yet to be conducted research; or (3) offers insights to the potential effect of outcomes of the researcher's study.

> Future research is located in the discussion chapter.

Example

In this example, the researcher speculates on future research based on using the study's methodology with different sets of participants.

Future Research

Recommendations for Future Research

After completing this study, several recommendations for future research were established. For instance, a parallel study could be conducted comparing two different groups of student leaders (e.g., leaders in a four-year leadership development program and student leaders who are not, or sorority and fraternity presidents, student organization presidents and dining services student managers, or perhaps a comparison of leaders and non-leaders to see if there really are differences between ESI and LPI, etc). The differences between samples would further identify the relationship between the two constructs and identify differences in leadership settings.

This study's methodology could be applied comparing a sample of student leaders with a sample of post-graduate leaders in a corporate setting. Interesting gender comparisons might be identified between leaders in corporate settings and college settings. Similarly, this study identified the relationships between Emotional-Social Intelligence and Student Leadership Practices, but did not establish causality between these variables. . . . This type of information would further identify the impacts or effects of one demographic variable on another. Researchers would be able to explore combinations of independent variables and determine which interactions have the most impact on ESI or student leadership practices. (Cavins, 2005, pp. 150–151)

Future Research Checklist

- ☐ Describe how future research links the study as part of the continuity of research on the topic.
- ☐ Identify how future research will address unanswered questions raised by the study.
- ☐ Offer speculation on how the study's methodology may be applied to different settings or participants.

G

GROUNDED THEORY

The researcher whose study involves a qualitative research design often refers to grounded theory. Grounded theory is a qualitative research methodology that focuses initially on the collection and careful analysis of data, especially qualitative data. From careful coding and interpretive practices, themes emerge and theory is generated (Blumer, 1969; Glaser & Strauss, 1967). The researcher presents grounded theory as a methodology and describes how she or he will use this methodology to collect data and generate new theory. The research also provides a rationale for using grounded theory with appropriate citations. Once data collection and data analysis are completed, the researcher inductively develops his or her theory and refers to the grounded theory methodology to discuss the new theory the data generated (Haig, 1995).

> Grounded theory is described in the introductory chapter, then is fully described as a methodology in the methodology chapter and discussed in the discussion chapter where the researcher presents his or her emerging theory.

Example

Note: In this example, the researcher provides a rationale for the use of grounded theory in this study.

Grounded Theory

In many ways, grounded theory is a good fit methodologically for the nature of the present study. The grounded theory method is useful for exploring under-theorized areas of investigation, such as inspiration in science, in which little data exists to generate or confirm hypotheses (Burk, 2005; Pidgeon, 1996). In addition, grounded theory is open to broader conceptions of science both in the topics that are open to investigation as well as in the methods it employs (Pidgeon, 1996), which makes it well suited for a study about the possible role of inspiration in science. (O'Grady, 2006, p. 32)

Grounded Theory Checklist

- ☐ Present grounded theory as a methodology.
- ☐ Provide a rationale for using grounded theory with appropriate citations.
- ☐ Describe the rigorous data analysis and interpretive processes used to generate theory.
- ☐ Present grounded theory in the discussion chapter and directly link it to the methodology.

H

HUMAN SUBJECTS (also Participants)

The Office for Protection from Research Risks defines a human subject as "a living individual about whom an investigator conducting research obtains (1) data through intervention or interaction with the individual, or (2) identifiable private information" (U.S. Department of Health and Human Services, 2005). Straightforwardly, human subjects are the individuals who are studied in the research. The researcher provides a clear and accurate description of the human subjects, often referred to as participants in the study. This description includes (1) participants' demographic characteristics, (2) criteria for selection as a participant, (3) detailed description of the involvement of participants, and (4) participant safeguards—especially if participants were from a vulnerable population. The researcher describes the precautions taken to protect the confidentiality of all participants. The researcher may indicate that the Institutional Review Board (IRB), consent forms, and full description of any treatment, experiment, questionnaire, survey, may be found in the appendix.

> The description of the human subjects is located in the methodology chapter.

Human Subjects Checklist

- ☐ Describe fully in the human subject application the demographics, contexts, level of involvement, and selection process.
- ☐ Describe the benefits and safeguards for the human subjects in the study.

- ☐ Identify the procedures taken to protect the confidentiality for human subjects.
- ☐ Make appropriate references to the IRB.
- ☐ Describe the research site and context where data are collected from human subjects.
- ☐ Place consent forms and other pertinent documents in the appendices.
- ☐ Explain fully the letter of consent and what involvement in the study will entail.
- ☐ See if your university mandates Human Subjects Training.

HUMAN SUBJECTS CLEARANCE

The researcher describes the process used to obtain human subjects clearance. She or he informs the reader that human subjects clearance was obtained through approval by the university's Institutional Review Board (IRB). The researcher is careful to describe the involvement of any human subjects and how the researcher obtained consent. The researcher pays special attention to describing the involvement of vulnerable populations and how she or he obtained consent of vulnerable populations.

> Sample human subjects clearance forms are placed in the appendices.

Human Subjects Clearance Checklist

- ☐ Describe the type and level of involvement of all human subjects in the study.
- ☐ Describe how consent was obtained from all human subjects involved in the study.
- ☐ Describe how protection was afforded to vulnerable populations in the study.
- ☐ Provide evidence of the IRB approval prior to initiation of the study.

HYPOTHESES

The researcher states his or her predictions for the outcome of the study in the form of a hypothesis that will be tested in the study. The researcher's hypothesis is speculative and a straightforward statement that seeks to measure the relationship among two or more variables. The researcher provides an operational definition of the theoretical constructs she or he seeks to test (Denkinger, 2007). She or he indicates if using a null hypothesis or an alternative hypothesis with the notation Ho for the null hypothesis or HA for the alternative hypothesis (Trochim, 2006).

> The hypotheses are initially identified in the introductory chapter, repeated in the methodology chapter, and restated verbatim in the results chapter.

Example

Hypotheses

Hypothesis 1: Participants with higher involvement (predisposition to attend graduate school) will score higher on a recall test based on information presented on a university Web site than those with lower involvement. (Martin, 2006, p. 47)

Hypothesis 2: Teacher education candidates significantly differ in their ethical sensitivity, by age, as measured by the Racial Ethical Sensitivity Test. (Maher, 2004, p. 7)

Hypotheses Checklist

- ☐ Formulate each hypothesis as a prediction of the study's outcome.
- ☐ Identify each hypothesis as a null hypothesis or an alternative hypothesis with appropriate notations.

I

IMPLICATIONS (see Implications for Future Research, Implications for Policy, and Implications for Practice)

IMPLICATIONS FOR FUTURE RESEARCH

The researcher reflects on the findings and makes a determination of the gaps that remain from her or his line of inquiry. She or he also discusses potential new lines of inquiry that emerged from the researcher's study. The researcher reflects on research antecedents, his or her research, and the future line of inquiry stimulated by the research. In reflecting on the antecedents leading to the research and the research she or he produced, the researcher thoughtfully and reflectively identifies lines of inquiry that advance the line of inquiry generated by her or his study.

> The implications for future research section is located in the discussion chapter.

Example

In this example, the researcher suggests both qualitative and quantitative research designs to further the line of inquiry pursued in the researcher's study.

Implications for Future Research

Implications for research include the following: increase qualitative and quantitative studies on staff nurses who work with baccalaureate student nurses in all areas of clinical practice. Descriptive studies related to the nurses' educational preparation are needed to determine if this variable has an influence on the nurses' professional socialization attitude toward students. Studies pertaining to faculty perceptions of staff nurses working with students are needed. Also, studies conducted on clinical education should include staff nurses' perceptions of nursing faculty. Quasi-experimental studies need to be conducted on the use of experimental clinical practice models for baccalaureate nursing education. In conclusion, future research is needed on the effects that collaborative educational reforms have on nurses, students, and faculty. (Hathorn, 2006, pp. 138–139)

Implications for Future Research Checklist

- ☐ Connect implications for future research to the research findings.
- ☐ Link implications for future research to the research study's antecedents to generate new lines of inquiry.
- ☐ Implications for future research are substantive and produce lines of inquiry firmly grounded in the tradition of the original line of inquiry.

IMPLICATIONS FOR POLICY

The researcher, as an educational researcher, understands the importance of his or her research on policy at the local, regional, national, and sometimes global levels. The product of the researcher's research is not policy and is never the final word on the direction of policy. The product of the researcher's study, however, adds to other research in making a case for policy decisions. The researcher makes a stronger case for the implications of the product of his or her research if supported by similar lines of inquiry. When the researcher describes how his or her research provides implications for policy, she or he places the research in the political arena. The researcher balances comments and has a foundation for all statements in the findings.

> The implications for policy are located in the discussion chapter.

Example

In this example, the researcher provides an introductory paragraph introducing two sections: implications for policy and implications for practice. The researcher addresses each topic in a separate subsection.

Implications for Policy

The findings of this study elicit several implications for policy and practice in the field of education, specifically in Pennsylvania. However, the following recommendations are based not only on the findings of this study. Additional influences include the review of mandated CPE for certification/licensure by state and the author's review of the literature of best practices in the field.

Implications for Practice

On November 23, 1999, Pennsylvania Governor Tom Ridge signed into law Act 1999-48 (24P.S. §§ 12-1205.1 et seq.), or Act 48, establishing CPE mandates for all certified educators. This legislation signifies a transition from optional CPE to mandatory CPE for all PA-certified educators, as previous requirements applied to only newly certified educators. As a result of the legislation, PDE established guidelines to regulate what the statutory language refers to as approved providers and to guide school districts in the development of their professional education plans.

Critics might argue that there is an absence of formal departmental policy regarding the tenets of CPE. The PDE guidelines established in the document, Act 48 Professional Education Plan Guidelines, provide assistance to school districts in meeting the requirements of Act 48. Flexibility in the guidelines proffered by PDE allowed school districts to interpret some criteria, as they deemed appropriate. A formal policy would outline specific requirements to which school districts must comply. (Craig, 2007, pp. 103–104)

Implications for Policy Checklist

- ☐ The implications for policy connect to your findings.
- ☐ The implications for policy are free of political rhetoric.
- ☐ The implications for policy provide specific directions for policy makers.

IMPLICATIONS FOR PRACTICE

The researcher, as an educational researcher, describes how the product of his or her research may constructively affect practice in the educational setting. The researcher also states under implications for practice (1) benefits of applying his or her research to practice, (2) benefits this research will provide for the practitioner in terms of increasing personal effectiveness and educational outcomes, and (3) the research's impact on those directly under the influence of the educational practitioner for whom the recommendation is made. Implications for practice are specific, describe actions, predict outcomes, and directly link to the researcher's findings.

The implications for practice are located in the discussion chapter.

Example

In this example, the researcher speculates on how the findings of the study might impact practice with Head Start children.

Implications for Practice

> Results from this study indicate that Head Start children responded positively to a universal primary prevention effort being implemented in Head Start classrooms in Alachua County, Florida. In particular, results from this study suggest that Head Start children benefited from a social skills curriculum (i.e., Second Step Violence Prevention Curriculum) that emphasized the acquisition of social-emotional skills (including empathy, social problem solving, and anger management techniques) that are likely to facilitate the transition to Kindergarten and provide foundational social and emotional competencies that are important for school success (Wentzel, 1991; Wentzel & Wigfield, 1998). This is based on the fact that these social-emotional competencies can be taught to young children and, more importantly, promoting foundational social and emotional skills early in life is considered an important step in preventing later aggression in children (Fray et al., 2000). (Wojtalewicz, 2004, p. 79)

Implications for Practice Checklist

- ☐ The implications for practice connect to the findings.
- ☐ The implications for practice provide specific actions leading to a cause-and-effect relationship.
- ☐ The implications for practice describe the benefit of the specific actions to the educational practitioner.

IMPORTANCE OF THE STUDY

The researcher describes the importance of his or her study at several levels: theory, methodology, practice, policy, and research. She or he describes how the research supported the theory undergirding the study. If the researcher uses grounded theory, she or he describes the theory that the research produced. In every case, the researcher connects the research to an existing or new theory, thus adding to the growing body of research related to the same theory. If the researcher proposes a new theory that deviates from traditional thought, she or he provides a thoughtful and substantive defense for the new theory. The researcher also describes the importance of the methodology that assisted in producing the study's results. She or he also may indicate how the methodology produced data that would not have been attained by employing another type of methodology.

The researcher describes the importance of the study to policy and practice in the discussion chapter section. The importance of the researcher's study to policy and practice is different from the implications of policy and practice. In the latter case, the implications are related to actions. In the former case, the researcher describes how the study contributes to the continual evolution of policy and practice.

> The importance of the study section is located in the discussion chapter.

Example

In this example, the researcher places the importance of the study in the discussion chapter to provide a rationale for the study's importance.

Importance of the Study

> The association among rural community, leadership, and community action is one that helps in linking theory and policy, as well as collectively serving as the basis for rural development policy in the United States over the past several decades. In fact, proponents of rural development at both the state and federal levels argue that community action and community leadership "must be at the forefront of effective programs to address rural problems" (Wilkinson, 1991, p. ix). A large number of individuals still inhabit rural communities today. Rural communities continue to make up an important part of the fabric of the American society and are still valued as something that should be promoted, defended and restored in social life (Wilkinson, 1986). As Flora and Flora (2004) point out, rural areas contribute many things to the nation, including "... (1) food security, (2) a sense of land stewardship that protects natural resources, (3) a value system connected to both the land and human relationship, and (4) protection of diversity" (p. 15). Therefore, it is important to rural people, and as an aspect of society itself, for rural communities to continue to fight and become viable and successful entities. (Wojtalewicz, 2004, p. 11)

Importance of the Study Checklist

- ☐ The importance of the study connects to the theory, methodology, practice, policy, and findings of the research.
- ☐ The importance of the study treats theory, methodology, practice, policy, and research as subsections of this section.
- ☐ The importance of the study addresses the "who cares" question.

INDEPENDENT VARIABLE

In quantitative research, the researcher operationally defines the independent variables prior to their measurement (usually in the dissertation proposal stage). She or he describes the effect of the independent variables in the study on the dependent variables (Babbie, 2004). The effect of the independent variable on the dependent variable is measured, and is reported in the researcher's dissertation. In essence, the independent variable acts on the dependent variable. It may include a specified treatment or indicators used in the following example, such as role occupant, role, role setting, and role orientation. The researcher remembers to describe any cause-and-effect relationship between the variables.

> The independent variables are located in the methodology or results chapters.

Example

In this example, the researcher provides an introductory paragraph naming the independent variables in the study. The researcher then describes each independent variable in the order listed in the introductory paragraph.

Independent Variables

The independent variables were subdivided into four primary categories: role occupant, role, role setting, and role orientation. Items on the survey related to the role occupant included personal demographic characteristics such as age, gender, marital status, parental status, number of years in athletic training education, year of and route to BOC certification, highest level of education, degree type, discipline of study, and previous employment and teaching experience.

Items on the survey related to the role included employment characteristics such as title, faculty rank, contract-type, contract length, number of years until review, teaching load per year, number of years at current institution, union affiliation, percentage of time spent in teaching, research, service, administration, clinical practice, and travel, and finally the number of hours worked per week.

Items on the survey related to the role setting included institutional characteristics such as school or college, division/department, degrees granted within department and athletic training program, number of hours required for degree, institutional affiliation/funding source (public/private), athletic affiliation, length of time accredited, number of years until re-accreditation, and program characteristics, including number of faculty, number of ACIs (on and off campus), number of affiliated sites, number of students, and faculty-to-student ratio.

Academic role orientation is the amount of emphasis placed on each area of faculty responsibility (teaching, research, and service). Role orientation has been further divided into seven areas: ideal orientation, actual orientation, institutional mission, needs of the profession, supervisor's orientation, colleagues' orientation, and role models' orientations. The individual's ideal and actual role orientations served as independent variables when examining role strain and the subscale items.

The degree to which a person's role orientation conforms to his or her role set members' expectations may be a cause of role strain. Therefore, role orientation congruity was also identified as an independent variable for examining role strain. Ideal role orientation congruity was classified according to ideal-actual congruity, ideal-institution congruity, ideal-supervisor congruity, and ideal-colleagues congruity. Actual role-orientation congruity was classified according to the actual-institutional, actual-supervisor, and actual-colleagues congruity. (Charles-Liscombe, 2007, pp. 18–20)

Independent Variables Checklist

- ☐ Describe fully each independent variable.
- ☐ Describe fully the operational definition of each independent variable.
- ☐ Describe the effects of the independent variables.
- ☐ Illustrate the independent variables in appropriate tables.

INSTITUTIONAL REVIEW BOARD (IRB)

Institutional Review Boards (IRBs) were established by the U.S. government to protect the rights and well-being of human subjects who will participate in research activities associated with the research study. The researcher fills out an IRB and is careful to describe (1) participant risks, if any; (2) participant benefits; (3) processes to ensure equitable selection to the study; (4) issues related to subject privacy and confidentiality; (5) any potential or real conflict of interests; (6) safety of the subjects; (7) process for informed consent; and (8) knowledge gained from the study. The researcher includes approval to conduct the study documentation, if necessary, from any agency where the study occurs. The approval is on agency letterhead and signed by the person responsible for making this decision. The researcher appends a copy of the approved IRB to the dissertation if the study requires the involvement of human subjects; the researcher also appends a copy of the consent forms.

> A copy of the approved IRB is placed in the appendices.

IRB Checklist

- ☐ Append a copy of the approved IRB to the dissertation.
- ☐ Append representative sample consent forms to the dissertation.
- ☐ Append a copy of the study site approval to the dissertation.
- ☐ Append a copy of protocols used in the study to the dissertation.
- ☐ Append copies of surveys, questionnaires, interviews, and other materials pertinent to the dissertation.

INSTRUMENTS

Many researchers refer to the term instrument to identify the means through which they collect data. Some researchers use the terms instrument and measures interchangeably. The instrument may take many forms. In general, instruments take the form of tests, observations or interviews, questionnaires and related scales, and direct collection of data (Black, 1999). The researcher provides strong empirical and theoretical support for the instruments used in the study. She or he describes the instrument and provides the reliability and validity of the instrument. A self-developed instrument is fully vetted and pilot-tested for face validity and theoretical support. The researcher also describes how the instrument was used in previous studies indicating settings, populations, and research results. The researcher assures the reader that the instruments used in his or her study will collect data that address the study's research questions or hypotheses.

> A description of the instruments used in the research study is located in the methodology chapter.

Example

The researcher identifies the instruments used to collect data in this study. The researcher provides a full description of each instrument in the dissertation. The full description of the instruments is excluded in this example due to its length.

> *Instrumentation*
>
> The researcher will use two instruments in this investigation: the Leader Effectiveness Adaptability Description (LEAD)-Self questionnaire and the Power Perception Profile (PPP)-Perception of Self questionnaire. Both instruments used for this study will involve self-reported responses by each participant. As with any survey research, it is assumed that all participants will respond honestly to the instruments they receive, and the data collected accurately reflect the perceptions of each participant regarding his or her leadership style and use of power. (Ates, 2003, p. 61)

Instruments Checklist

- ☐ The instruments used in the study have strong empirical and theoretical support.
- ☐ Describe how the instruments used in the study collect data that addresses the research questions or hypotheses.
- ☐ Any self-developed instrument is fully vetted and pilot-tested for face validity and theoretical support. See *pilot testing* for further explanation.

INTERNAL VALIDITY

The researcher describes how his or her study mitigated threats to the study's internal validity. The researcher describes the relationship between the variables in the study from a causal viewpoint. Internal validity allows the researcher to make valid conclusions about the causal effects between the study's variables. She or he also makes a case that variable *a* had a causal effect on variable *b* without the interference of any unknown variable. She or he describes how the research design strengthened the probability that any cause-and-effect relationship took into account data collected from control and test groups (Trochim, 2006). If the researcher is making an inference from case study research, she or he describes how all other possible rival explanations have been explored (Yin, 2003).

> A description of the internal validity is located in the methodology chapter.

Example

In this example, the researcher describes how the research's internal validity was protected in this qualitative study.

> *Internal Validity*
>
> Techniques used to establish internal validity for this study included prolonged engagement or time in the field. The researcher was present in the fifth-grade EIP classrooms for at least three hours per week over an eight-month span. This allowed repeated observations and a deeper understanding of the kinds of relationships that developed in the classes. These understandings allowed theories to emerge, which were confirmed or disconfirmed by participants. This process of confirming/disconfirming is often referred to as "member checking" in qualitative literature.
>
> Member checks are important because they provide the researcher with additional data to use in developing theory. Additional measures taken to address potential threats to internal validity included the pilot study, establishing relationships with participants prior to initial interviews and creating an atmosphere of trust through disclosure and honesty about the reasons for the research. Dependability and confirmability of data are additional criteria for establishing internal validity in qualitative studies. These concepts refer to the process of describing data collection procedures in very explicit and detailed methods, which permit others to gain understanding in enough depth that the intervention can be replicated (Lincoln & Guba, 1985). (Jaffe, 2006, pp. 61–62)

Internal Validity Checklist

- ☐ Describe how threats to the internal validity of the study were managed.
- ☐ Describe how claims to a cause-and-effect relationship did not have external interference.
- ☐ Identify other rival explanations for claimed cause-and-effect relationships.

INTERVIEWS

The interview method is commonly used to collect data in qualitative research. The researcher describes the participant as a member of the unit of analysis, the participant's context and role, protocols associated with the interview, and any confounding factors that caused the researcher to alter the originally designed protocols. The researcher protects the interviewee's confidentiality. Interview data are analyzed using appropriate qualitative data analysis procedures. Rich and descriptive quotations from the interview are reported verbatim in support of the findings.

> A description of interview protocols, participants, and interview context are located in the methodology chapter. Quotations from interview data are reported in the findings and results chapter.

Example

In this example, the researcher describes how the researcher conducted in-depth interviews in this study. The researcher indicates that interview protocols are located in the appendices.

Interviews

Survey research helped to provide the baseline data to begin to describe the experiences of Black evaluators. Qualitative inquiry, with its focus on holistic perspective and interpretation, provided a clearer understanding of the population. Qualitative research focuses on three major genres (1) individual lived experience, (2) society and culture, and (3) language and communication (Marshall & Rossman, 1999). The focus of this study was to understand the individual lived experiences of Black evaluators. It is the researcher's belief that qualitative data can yield a better understanding of the evaluator experience by allowing evaluators to speak for themselves.

Given the experiences of the interviewees and their breadth of knowledge, a face-to-face interview strategy was initially viewed as the way to proceed. However, for the same reasons as mentioned above, an interview guide was developed to assist in standardizing interviews, as well as to compensate for the researcher's novice interviewer status. Patton (2002) wrote that the "combined strategy offers the interviewer flexibility in probing and in determining when it is appropriate to explore certain subjects in greater depth, or even to pose questions about new areas of inquiry that were not originally anticipated in the interview instrument's development" (p. 347). All interviewees were asked to complete the online questionnaire.

An interview guide was developed to assist in structuring the discussion with each of the four interviewees. The interview protocol developed consisted of four sections: (1) background/experience, (2) cultural competence in evaluation, (3) race in evaluation, and (4) mentoring initiatives. These categories were developed to coincide with the questions developed for the survey. These categories represent areas where more in-depth information was desired. The interview guide can be found in Appendix B. (Bertrand, 2006, pp. 41–42)

Interview Data Checklist

- ☐ Protect the confidentiality of interviewees.
- ☐ Place a copy of the interview protocols in the appendices.
- ☐ Demonstrate how data collected from the interviews link to the research questions and hypothesis.

INTRODUCTION (also Organization of the Chapter)

Each chapter to the dissertation has an introduction. In many cases, the introduction is limited to a single opening paragraph that provides a blueprint to the chapter. The introduction to the chapter succinctly states the purpose of the chapter in the first sentence. The researcher then describes the essential components that compose the chapter. These components become the headers for the chapter, forming a chapter outline. They are presented in logical order to the reader. In some cases, this is called the organization of the chapter. Chapter 1 is the only chapter that does not follow this pattern. Chapter 1 is the introductory chapter to the dissertation. Refer to Chapter 1, Chapter 2, Chapter 3, Chapter 4, and Chapter 5 for the components commonly found in the chapters.

> Chapter 1 is the introductory chapter to the dissertation. All other chapters open with an introductory paragraph.

Example

In this example, the researcher begins the chapter with an introduction to the literature review chapter. The researcher writes a single opening paragraph that provides a blueprint to the chapter.

Introduction

Review of the Literature

> This chapter begins with literature germane to appreciative inquiry and humanistic psychology related to peak experiences of teachers in a teaching and learning context. The purpose of this review is to provide an understanding of the previous research in this area. I will first discuss my conceptual framework. I will then discuss my theoretical frameworks. Next, I will identify competing perspectives, and conclude with a review and synthesis of the relevant empirical research. (Hummel, 2007, p. 16)

Introduction Checklist

- ☐ Each chapter of the dissertation has an introduction paragraph.
- ☐ With the exception of the introductory chapter, the introduction to the remaining chapters is an overview of the chapter.

INTRODUCTORY CHAPTER (see Chapter 1)

K

KEY TERMS (see Definition of Terms)

L

LIMITATIONS

The researcher describes the possible and real weaknesses to his or her research design in the limitations section. Creswell (2002) suggests that the researcher examine the methodology, data collection methods, and analysis procedures for possible limitations. The limitations described by the researcher are those that may or did affect the study's validity or findings (Rubin & Babbie, 2004). The limitations section of the dissertation addresses the researcher's awareness of the shortcomings to his or her research design and methodological approach to the study, thus adding to the researcher's credibility.

> A description of the research study's limitations is located in the introductory chapter. Limitations that occur during the conduct of the study are described in the discussion chapter.

Example

In this example, the researcher describes limitations as a reflection on the study in the discussion chapter. The researcher indicates the study's shortcomings and suggestions for strengthening future inquiry using a similar research design.

Limitations

There are several limitations to this study. First, since data were drawn from a single highly selective Research I institution, it cannot be generalized to other institutions. Second, the data for this study is skewed because the insti-

> tution was highly homogeneous in comparison with other institutions. Third, the instrument used, the SDTLI, tests only three out of seven of Chickering's vectors. Nevertheless, the SDTLI has been extremely reliable in test-retest correlations. Winston and Miller (1987) and Winston (1990) confirmed after several test-retest periods that range from two to twenty weeks that the SDTLI is stable over time; Pearson's Correlations ranged from .70 to .87. Since the test has been shown to be so reliable, there is little room to make significant deviations. However, since this study is a longitudinal study conducted over a period of four years, the test-retest limitation may not be applicable. Fourth, the freshman year SDTLI score was gathered in late October of the freshman year. Since most students had integrated into their new surroundings during the first few weeks of entrance, the data for the freshman SDTLI would have been more reliable for this study if it had been gathered during students' orientation week. Fifth, since this study is based on data gathered only in the students' freshman and senior years, and not in their sophomore and junior years, there is no data on students who did not remain in the institution. Did they transfer, drop out, or graduate early? The study may have been further enhanced if it also included a sophomore year survey, a junior year survey, and a senior year survey. Thus, further details could have been gathered on the changes, or lack thereof, of the students' perceptions of the institution throughout their college careers. . . . It is strongly recommended to have future studies that gather data from all four years of college in order to obtain less skewed data on the influence of social integration. (Lien, 2002, pp. 46–47)

Limitations Checklist

- ☐ Each research design limitation is a potential weakness related to the theoretical perspective or research methodology.
- ☐ Each research design weakness is recognized and placed in the limitation section.

LIST OF FIGURES

The researcher follows guidelines of the graduation school or department in his or her university related to the placement and format for the list of figures. In general, a list of figures is provided in numerical sequence indicating the number of the figure and its location in the dissertation.

> The list of figures is located after the table of contents.

Example

In this example, the researcher lists the figure number in the left-hand column and the page number in the far right-hand column. The researcher places the figure title after the figure number.

List of Figures (Dondanville, 2005, p. ix)

List of Figures Checklist

- ☐ Each figure is listed in numerical order.
- ☐ The list of figures follows graduate school and department norms.

LIST OF TABLES

The researcher follows the guidelines of the graduation school or department in his or her university related to the placement and format for the list of tables. In general, a list of tables is provided in numerical sequence indicating the number of the table and its location in the dissertation.

> The list of tables is located after the table of contents.

Example

In this example, the researcher lists the table number in the left-hand column and the page number in the far right-hand column. The researcher places the table title after the table number.

List of Tables (D. Brown, 2006, p. viii)

List of Tables Checklist

- ☐ Each table in the list of tables is listed in numerical order.
- ☐ The list of tables follows graduate school and department norms.

LITERATURE REVIEW (also Chapter 2)

The dissertation's literature review is composed of several parts and corresponding subparts (Calabrese, 2006). The literature review begins with an introduction paragraph that offers a blueprint to the chapter. Several sections compose the literature review: (1) conceptual framework, (2) theoretical framework, (3) competing or alternative theory, (4) search methodology for identifying the relevant empirical research, (5) themes or findings from the review of the relevant empirical research, and (6) a summary of the chapter.

The researcher presents the body of the literature review as a chronological or thematic description of the relevant empirical research. In this section, the researcher includes (1) search rationale and methodology, (2) description of the logic used in selecting or rejecting research to be reported in the literature review, and (3) a critical synthesis of the research that presents a balanced view of the research providing point and counterpoint, as well as exposing gaps in the research. In assessing the relevant empirical research, the researcher identifies limitations in existing studies that focus on the study's methodological and research design. In essence, the literature review provides a historical overview of the researcher's theoretical perspectives and relevant empirical research that leads to generation of new research questions requiring further inquiry (Taylor & Procter, 2008).

The literature review is located in the literature review chapter.

Example

In this example, the researcher presents a brief introduction to Chapter 2, identifying the essential components to be discussed in the literature review chapter. The example presents the introduction and organization of the researcher's literature review.

> ***Literature Review***
>
> This chapter presents a review of literature related to effective counselor characteristics (ECC), admission requirements, and procedures. First, research on the characteristics of effective counselors is presented. Second, graduate college admission requirements and procedures are examined. Third, professional development and standards of preparation are investigated.
>
> These three areas relate to the threefold purpose of this study, which is to identify effective counselor characteristics (ECC), describe existing admission requirements, and develop a framework for a standardized set of admission requirements for assessing prospective counseling students. This study is based on the fact that (a) many aren't sure, and cannot agree on, what the characteristics of effective counselors are or should be; (b) personal-emotional characteristics of effective counselors are usually minimally addressed or absent in admissions; and (c) there is not a framework for a standard set of admission requirements. (Smith, 2004, p. 23)

Literature Review Checklist

- ☐ The literature review fully describes the researcher's conceptual framework.
- ☐ The literature review contains the researcher's search methodology for the relevant empirical research.
- ☐ The literature review provides a rationale for including or excluding empirical research.
- ☐ The presentation of the relevant empirical research in the literature review is in a thematic, chronological, or other logical order.

M

MAJOR FINDINGS

Researchers describe their major findings and distinguish them from minor findings. In quantitative dissertations, the major findings are linked to the dependent variables. In qualitative research, the major findings are linked to the overall research questions that guided the study. The determination of major findings is subjective, yet informed by the strength of the researcher's data analysis. The researcher describes major findings with sufficient support to provide criteria for judgment by other researchers determining if they would reach the same conclusion regarding the major findings.

The major findings are located in the findings and results chapter.

Example

In this example, the researcher first refers to major findings in the abstract with a summary of the major findings. The researcher elaborates on the major findings in Chapter 4, the Results Chapter.

Major Findings

> Major findings from this study concluded that teacher participants recognize professional development as the common thread that motivates teachers, improves their sense of efficacy, assists them in successful curriculum implementation, and heightens their awareness of the need to improve teaching practices and the need to become student-centered and improve student learning. Principal participants concurred with teacher

> participants, and recognize the role leaders play in motivating teachers to become actively engaged in professional learning activities. (Bennett, 2007, p. ii)

Major Findings Checklist

- ☐ Major findings are fully supported by the data and data analysis.
- ☐ The data analysis was substantive and accurate, providing assurance in the selection of the major findings.
- ☐ With the same data and analysis, other researchers would also select the same major findings.

MEASURES

The term measures may have multiple meanings in a dissertation. In one sense, it may be subsumed under the topic instruments. It may be used as a noun indicating the measure is a system or scale. Measure may also be used as a noun indicating the degree or quality of the object measured. Also, measure may be used as a verb when the researcher says, "I measured the differences in test scores." In general, in a dissertation measures reference (1) a system, (2) a scale, or (3) an action that assesses outcome, reliability, or validity.

> The description of measures is mentioned in the introduction chapter and again in the methodology chapter.

Example

In this example, the researcher describes the instrument's outcome of the intention of the instrument used in the study.

Measures

> The BASIS-A (Wheeler et al., 1993) measures five life-style themes: Belonging-Social Interest (BSI), Going Along (GA), Taking Charge (TC), Wanting Recognition (WR), and Being Cautious (BC). It also has five subscales that help to broaden the interpretation of the BASIS-A profile:

> Harshness (H), Entitlement (E), Liked by All (L), Striving for Perfection (P), and Softness (S). Internal consistency reliability of the five BASIS-A scales ranges from .82 to .87. Test-retest reliability shows a moderate level of stability across scales (Wheeler et al.). The BASIS-A has been used successfully in a variety of clinical applications (Wheeler, 1996). (Suprina, 2005, pp. 34–35)

Measures Checklist

- ☐ The measures used in the research are strongly supported in the literature.
- ☐ Fully describe how the research measures used by the researcher provide sufficient and accurate data to address the research questions and hypotheses.
- ☐ The measure has theoretical support, reliability, and face validity.
- ☐ Fully vet any self-developed metric.
- ☐ Pilot test any self-developed metric.

METHODOLOGY (also Chapter 3)

The researcher uses the methodology chapter to describe procedures in her or his research to collect data that address the research questions and hypotheses. This operational plan is the strategy behind her or his research approach, choice of line of inquiry, and methods to collect data. In essence, the researcher's description of the methodology provides the framework and rationale for selected choices of methods (Crotty, 2003). A subset of the methodology is the researcher's methods that will be used to collect data to address the research questions and hypotheses. Included in the description are confounding issues that arose during the collection of data. The researcher first addresses those issues she or he foresaw, and then addresses the confounding issues that were not predicted at the onset of the study.

> The methodology is first described in the introductory chapter and then wholly in the methodology chapter.

Example 1

In this example, the researcher provides an overview of the methodology in the introduction chapter. Later, in the methodology chapter, the researcher provides a complete description of the methodology and its subparts.

Overview of Methodology

> Very few paraeducators persist from the MTEC informational sessions to the teacher education program admission process. . . . A phenomenological study devoted to understanding their lived experiences was deemed appropriate for this question because very few studies exploring paraeducators' experiences exist. A phenomenological study describes the meaning of the lived experiences for several individuals about a concept or the phenomenon (Creswell, 1998, p. 51). Phenomenology seeks to gain a deeper understanding of the nature or meaning of our everyday experiences (Van Manen, 1997, p. 9). This qualitative method of research is appropriate for describing the thoughts, feelings, and actions of these five minority women's experiences in their career transition from paraeducator to professional teacher. (White, 2002, p. 5)

Example 2

In this example, the researcher identifies the purpose of the study, unit of analysis, and the methodology used to collect data.

Research Methodology

> The purpose of this study was to uncover accomplished elementary school teachers' perspectives on how high-stakes testing influences instructional decisions and professionalism. To further define this study, accomplished teachers, by their designation as National Board Certified Teachers, were interviewed to gain their perspectives to determine if their instructional decisions and sense of professionalism were influenced by high-stakes testing. The participants in this study included six accomplished teachers selected from five elementary schools in a single suburban school system. A qualitative case study approach was used to discover the accomplished

teachers' experiences and their perspectives about these experiences. In the study by Pedulla et al. (2003), they indicated, "only by listening to what teachers tell us is happening as a result of these state testing programs can we be confident that they are having the intended effect" (p. 123).

This chapter included the research questions, the theoretical framework that guided the research, a description of the research design and rationale for the study, the data sources, an overview of the analysis of the data, and the limitations of the study. (Schulz, 2005, p. 59)

Methodology Checklist

- ☐ The methodology fully describes the rationale for the choices of methods.
- ☐ The methodology indicates the direction of inquiry for the choices of methods and intended outcomes of the research.
- ☐ The methodology includes the subset of methods used to collect data (see methods).

METHODS

The methods are a subset of the methodology. Methods are the specific procedures the researcher used to collect data (Crotty, 2003). The researcher identifies each method and describes how the method was used in the study. She or he links the method to research questions and hypotheses to provide a rationale for its use to collect relevant data. The researcher provides appropriate citations of the method. In cases where the researcher uses a method not commonly seen in his or her line of inquiry, she or he provides definitions with appropriate citations.

> The methods are located in the methodology chapter.

Example

In this example, the researcher identified the methods used to collect data in the study.

Methods

> A variety of methods were used to gather data. Focus groups were held with school counselors. Questionnaires were administered to fourteen randomly selected students. Thirty-four teachers were randomly selected to participate in a focus group and complete Likert-type items on questionnaires. Three elementary school principals were randomly selected to participate in individual structured interviews, while thirteen of the remaining principals were asked to complete a questionnaire with the same items found on the teacher's questionnaire. (Loop, 1997, p. 45)

Methods Checklist

- ☐ The application of each method is fully described.
- ☐ Each method is related to the research questions and hypotheses.
- ☐ The methodology includes the subset of methods used to collect data (see methodology).

MODEL DEVELOPMENT

The researcher describes any models developed for data collection. In doing so, the researcher carefully describes the theory supporting the model, criteria used to measure the data regarding the dependent variable, and the effects of modifying the independent variables on the dependent variable. The researcher provides (1) information regarding what data were actually collected, (2) research design, (3) criteria used to ensure that the research is valid (Schensul, LeCompte, & Schensul, 1999). If the researcher builds a research model, she or he references appropriate theory, historical evolution of research regarding the model's genesis to its present state, and the seminal researchers involved in the evolution of the model. The researcher also accurately describes the steps taken in designing, developing, and testing the model. Models are used to explain findings and results. The researcher may provide a model of forces, contexts, and populations that affected the outcome of the study as a way of explaining the findings and results.

> A description of model development is located in the methodology chapter. If it is used to explain the findings and results, it is also located in the discussion chapter.

Example

In this example, the researcher describes the logic and process for model development for the study reported in this dissertation. Earlier in this researcher's dissertation, the researcher described the background to the model's development.

Model Development

A giant-sized conceptual model drawing was placed on a wall and was first thought to be a logical place to begin to try to discover relationships between the categories. Large-type versions of each of the codes and propositional statements were created and then cut into strips. The next step was to place them on the wall-sized model in different patterns and groupings. During this phase of the research, it became clear that the model did not meet the needs of the emerging data. The model did not address what the data seemed to be suggesting, that being that there was more to the interactive relationships than what had been determined in the model. Further, the school, its staff, programs, and practices needed to be more of a contributing factor in the equation and was somewhat underrepresented in the original model. With several frustrating days lapsing with no progress toward finding relationships, a concept emerged about the relationship of the data to the model. It seemed that between the overlapping relationships and the engagement of students there was an intermediary step that was both a result of interaction and a catalyst for engagement. It was with this thought that coded categorical relationships began to emerge and the process of discovery became somewhat meaningful and rather exciting. Chapter 4 includes a thorough discussion of the themes and ideas that emerged from the coded categorical data. A new wall chart was ultimately developed with larger themes borne from the data as headings. A copy of that chart appears in Appendix N. (Constantino, 2002, p. 46)

Model Development Checklist

- ☐ Describe each aspect of the research model.
- ☐ Link the dependent and independent variables in the research model.
- ☐ Provide the reader with the antecedents to the genesis and evolution of the research model.

MODIFICATIONS

The researcher reports any modifications made to research instruments such as tests and surveys or the protocols or procedures in their implementation. She or he provides a rationale and research support for the modifications with appropriate citations. In some cases, especially in qualitative research, the research design, research questions, or methodology evolve and new theories, questions, and hypotheses are tested (Merriam, 2001). In this case, the researcher describes how her or his study evolved describing data that caused the modification of the research design, research questions, or methodology.

> A description of the research study's modifications is located in the methodology chapter and their impact is described in the discussion chapter.

Example

In this example, the researcher describes data sources, then uses the data collected from the data sources to make decisions related to modifications.

Modifications

The researcher will transcribe the interviews. This will provide an assessment of potential problems with the research questions, technique, field-note

> strategies, or recording equipment. The participants will provide artifacts that support ideas they express. Field notes will be written during the pilot study that will contain descriptive data of what was observed and researcher comments on data and the project itself. The field-note-taking guide is in Appendix D. The researcher will discuss these results with his committee to help identify necessary modifications to the study. (Gross, 2006, p. 83)

Modifications Checklist

- ☐ Fully describe each modification.
- ☐ A substantive rationale for each modification accompanies the description of the modification.

N

NEED FOR THE STUDY (also Rationale for the Study)

The need for the study is the researcher's rationale that the study is original research on a substantive issue. She or he provides the context, background, and theoretical underpinnings for the research. The researcher also provides evidence that the study will contribute to the body of knowledge regarding the topic of study by exposing gaps in the research.

> The need for the study is located in the introductory chapter.

Example

In this example, the researcher makes a case for the importance of conducting this study by describing the benefit derived from conducting the study.

Need for the Study

Currently, no instrument has been developed that assesses residents' perceptions of equity in the context of the allocation and distribution of public services. It has been observed that, "Because recreation and parks departments typically provide a wide array of services, from maintenance of open space to social service programs, there are likely to be a diversity of equity concepts associated with them" (Wicks & Crompton, 1989, p. 171). It is the intent of this dissertation to develop a valid and reliable instrument that will assess residents' perceptions of equity in the allocation of publicly provided park and recreation services. Information ascertaining residents'

> perceptions of equity can be used by elected officials and park and recreation administrators to guide their decisions on the allocation of resources for service delivery and ultimately enable them to distribute their departments' services in accordance with stake holders' allocation desires. The end result would be a more equitable allocation and distribution of public park and recreation facilities. (West, 2002, pp. 8–9)

Need for the Study Checklist

- ☐ The need for the study identifies and describes gaps in the research.
- ☐ The need for the study provides evidence indicating that the study will focus on a substantive issue.
- ☐ The need for the study makes a case that the study is substantive by providing meaningful and relevant data.

NULL HYPOTHESIS

The null hypothesis indicates the researcher's theory that there are no differences between variables. If the researcher uses a null hypothesis, she or he is careful to state the null hypothesis in terms of predicting that there will be no relationship between groups or variables (Polgar & Thomas, 2000). The researcher's analysis of study data indicates if the null hypothesis was rejected. The null hypothesis is stated as H0.

> The null hypothesis is first stated in the introductory chapter, repeated in the methodology chapter, and restated in the results chapter.

Example

In this example, the researcher states the null hypothesis for one of the study's research questions. The researcher then describes the statistical analysis procedures used to determine whether the null hypothesis should be rejected. In the example, the researcher finds that there is no significant difference, thus upholding the null hypothesis.

Null Hypothesis

The null hypothesis for question #5 is that there is no significant difference between male faculty members' levels of involvement in institutional governance and female faculty members' levels of involvement. To answer question #5, I used two-tailed t-tests to examine the differences between the means of two groups, male faculty members and female faculty members, on the self-reported level of involvement. Then I followed with additional t-tests to determine the differences between the means of male faculty members and female faculty members on the scale of involvement variable. The obtained probability statistic (p value) rejected or failed to reject the null hypothesis m. (Campbell, 2003, p. 52)

Null Hypothesis Checklist

- ☐ The null hypothesis asserts no differences will be found between variables or groups.
- ☐ The null hypothesis uses the notation H0.
- ☐ The null hypothesis is restated in the methodology and results chapters.
- ☐ The researcher's analysis of study data indicates if the null hypothesis was accepted or rejected.

O

OBJECTIVES OF THE STUDY (see Research Goals)

OBSERVATIONS (also Field Notes)

The researcher describes how she or he used either direct or indirect observation as a data collection tool. She or he describes how the use of observation facilitated the understanding of situations, behaviors, or physical space (Evaluation Research Team, 2008). Field notes are often the result of the researcher's observations from the research setting. According to Merriam (2001), field notes may contain the researcher's descriptions of people, their context, and activities with which they are involved. Field notes may be (1) direct quotations from participants taken by the researcher, (2) the researcher's comments taken at the research setting that are explanatory or theory-based in nature, or (3) reflections made immediately after the observation. In general, field notes are placed in the appendices and are used as supportive evidence in the dissertation. The researcher may provide descriptive supporting evidence for the case she or he is making in the field notes. In any case, the researcher adds only relevant field notes to the dissertation.

> The observations and field notes are described in the methodology chapter. They may be used as a source of rich and descriptive data in the results chapter. Examples of observations and field notes may be placed in the appendices.

Example

In this example, the researcher describes how field notes as observations were maintained and used during data collection and in data analysis.

Observations

> Each member of the research team maintained a set of [observations] field notes during the data collection and analysis phases of the study. These field notes were used to help research team members reflect on reactions to data that they encountered. By maintaining these field notes, research team members were able to examine the data and record observations and impressions. The field notes were used to identify recurring themes that were later used in the development of concepts, categories, and higher order categories. Additionally, the field notes allowed research team members to identify potential sources of bias. (Gonzales, 2006, p. 47)

Observation Checklist

- ☐ The researcher maintains rich descriptions of his or her observations of people, their context, and activities.
- ☐ The researcher adds only relevant observations to the dissertation.
- ☐ The researcher records, analyzes, and maintains record of observations in a safe repository.

OPERATIONAL DEFINITIONS

The researcher states the operational definitions for understanding theoretical and methodological approaches as well as correctly interpreting the analyzed data. The researcher defines the operational definitions by using unambiguous language that describes the specific focus of the data-gathering event. She or he uses operational definitions consistently throughout the dissertation. The researcher takes appropriate precautions to ensure the validity and reliability of the operational definitions (Robinson, 2007).

> A description of the operational definitions is located in the methodology chapter.

Example

In this example, the researcher defines the use of essential terms. The researcher defines each term to precisely indicate how it is used in the researcher's study.

Operational Definitions

Admission review (Initial)—Each application was reviewed by two admission counselors to determine a subjective score that was added to the objective score (Office of Admissions and Records, 2001a). If there was a substantial disparity between the scores awarded, a third review was conducted. After the distribution of all scores was evaluated, a preliminary cutoff score was determined. This score allowed room for some additional admission decisions to be made among those students immediately below that score in one last process.

Educational level of parents—In the application, students reported the parents' educational levels. Students were assigned a score of 0–6. The higher of the two parents' scores was used for this study.

Employment—Students reported their work history in the application. Based on the average hours per week worked and number of months employed, they were assigned a score. The more hours that the student reported having worked, particularly hours during the school year, the higher the student's score was on a scale of 0–9.

Ethnicity/race—Students reported their race/ethnicity. The options included White (not Hispanic origin), Hispanic, African American, American Indian, Asian or Pacific Islander, and Other. Students in this study could only check one of the options, and some students chose to leave all options blank. This information was not visible to admission counselors during the admission review process. (Boyd, 2004, pp. 8–9)

Operational Definitions Checklist

- ☐ Operational definitions are explicit and fully described.
- ☐ Operational definitions have a high degree of validity and reliability.
- ☐ Operational definitions are definitions that are measured in the analysis.
- ☐ Operational definitions are used in the same consistent manner throughout the dissertation.

ORGANIZATION OF THE CHAPTER (see Introduction)

ORGANIZATION OF THE STUDY (also Dissertation Outline)

The organization of the study is the summary section of the introductory chapter. In the summary section, the researcher describes the chapter's primary intent in the first sentence of the summary paragraph. As the researcher describes the chapter's primary intent, she or he lists the components included in this introductory chapter (see Chapter 1). The researcher then provides the reader with a brief, one-sentence description of each of the subsequent chapters.

> The organization of the study is located at the conclusion of the introductory chapter.

Example

In this example, the researcher closes Chapter 1 with an overview of organization of the remaining chapters in the dissertation. The researcher presents a succinct statement for each of the four remaining chapters of the dissertation.

> ***Organization of the Study***
>
> Chapter 1 provides an introduction, indicating a purpose and need for the study. Chapter 2 discusses teaching as it relates to student learning, the evaluation process as it relates to the district's expectation of teachers, and the selection practices used by school personnel. Chapter 3 describes the methodology of the study, detailing the process used to collect and analyze the data. Chapter 4 presents the data and the statistical analysis of the results. Chapter 5 provides a summary of the study's results, the conclusions reached, and recommendations for the future. (Wede, 1996, p. 7)

Organization of the Study Checklist

- ☐ The organization of the study contains a one-sentence summary statement of the introductory chapter's intention.
- ☐ The organization of the study restates each of the components covered in the introductory chapter.
- ☐ The organization of the study states the intent of each subsequent chapter in the dissertation.

OUTCOMES AND IMPLICATIONS OF THE STUDY

The phrase outcomes and implications of the study, seen in some dissertations, is a catch-all summary term that includes implications for future research, implications for policy, implications for practice, and importance of the study. Refer to those terms for a definition of outcomes and implications of the study.

> The outcomes and implications of the study section is located in the discussion chapter.

OVERVIEW OF THE RESEARCH DESIGN (see Overview of the Study)

OVERVIEW OF THE STUDY (also Overview of the Research Design)

The overview of the study is generally presented as a precursor to the researcher's study. The researcher uses the overview of the study to state intentions for conducting the study. As such, it contains a summary statement of the context, background, theoretical perspectives, problem statement, research questions, and methodology. The overview of the study may also serve as a summary of the study once the research is completed (see following example).

Many researchers use the term overview as a way to introduce the study or subparts of the study such as "overview of the research design." The central point is the presentation of information that previews a substantive discussion that follows the overview.

> The overview of the study is located in the introductory chapter. Some researchers place it in the abstract. In some cases, researchers substitute the term overview for introduction.

Example

In this example, the researcher provides a brief summary of the study reported in this dissertation.

Overview of the Study

> This study was conducted in one section of a college-level elementary probability and statistics course at a midwestern university during the ten-week, spring quarter of 2003. All the sections of this course were large (initial enrollment of 56 students in the observed section) and primarily lecture in structure. Qualitative research methods were employed to make visible the covert thought processes probability and statistics students had while learning and solving individual and group problems. Students were observed in their class setting, and seven of the students were purposefully selected to explain the notes they took during one of the classes. Then the selected students were asked to solve, out loud, two statistical problems, one alone as the researcher observed and one with a group of the participating students. All of the students could not be interviewed, which eliminates generalizing the results to all statistics students. The process of selecting the interviewees, however, did provide a sample representative of the students in this course section. The interviews were taped, transcribed, coded for evidence of metacognitive behavior in these seven human subjects, and analyzed. Four common themes emerged from the individual profiles of the interviewed participants: novice versus expert problem solving, statistics as a viable subject, self-reporting, and the cognitive-metacognitive framework. (Rysz, 2004, pp. 12–13)

Overview of the Study Checklist

- ☐ The overview of the study contains the essential components leading to the implementation of the study.
- ☐ The overview of the study informs the reader of the researcher's intentions for implementing the study.
- ☐ The overview of the study is a concise "executive summary" of the essential components of the research conducted by the researcher.

P

PARTICIPANT CHARACTERISTICS

The researcher provides descriptions or data relevant to all pertinent characteristics of the study's participants. These characteristics could include (1) age, (2) gender, (3) years of experience, (4) levels of education, and (5) any other items that situate the participants in the study. Depending on the research design, the researcher may present demographic data in tables, narrative, or both. The researcher may feel that the context of the study is important to link to the participant characteristics. In doing so, the researcher uses the context to add richness to the participant characteristics. The researcher, for example, may be studying the effects of in-school suspension on student achievement. In this case, the description of the in-school suspension environment would be beneficial for understanding the participants, whether students or supervisors.

> A description of participant characteristics is generally first placed in the methodology chapter and repeated in the findings and results chapter.

Example

In this example, the researcher provides a general description of the study's participants, then moves toward specificity referencing data in a table.

Participant Characteristics

Study participants included undergraduate students 18 years of age or older. All participants were undergraduates enrolled at a large southeastern university during the spring semester of 2007. Data collection procedures produced 369 usable surveys. Of the 392 surveys completed by participants, 23 were discarded because of excessive missing data.

Age, Gender, Race and Class: Table 4-1 provides a summary of participants by age, gender, race and ethnicity, and academic class. A large percentage of the participants were aged 20–21 (n = 181, 46.2%) and 18–19 (n = 152, 38.8%) with only a small percentage aged 22–23 (n = 47, 12%), 24–25 (n = 1, .3%) and over 25 (n = 7, 1.8%).

The final sample had a greater number of female participants (n = 315, 81%), than male participants (n = 72, 19%). Most participants were White (68.6%) and a small percentage sampled were Black/African American (10.2%), Asian (8.7%), Hispanic (7.9%), and Other (3.1%). This is not a representation of ethnicities in the United States, but it is similar to undergraduate enrollment during 2007.

In this sample, males and Hispanics are underrepresented based on university demographics for undergraduates, but the other groups are similar to enrollment in 2007 (female = 54%; male = 46%; Whites = 66%; Hispanic = 13%; Black/African American = 9.6%; Asian 7.26%). (Batia, 2007, p. 57)

Participant Characteristics Checklist

- ☐ Participant characteristics are explicit and accurate.
- ☐ Participant characteristics are referenced in a table in the appropriate chapter.
- ☐ Participant characteristics provide meaningful demographic data.

PARTICIPANT SAMPLE

The participant sample is the larger group from which the study's participants are drawn. The study's participants (see *sample*) are selected from the participant sample and mirror the demographic make-up of the participant sample. The researcher describes the attributes of the participant sample and provides a rationale for the sample. For example, the researcher may be studying teacher attrition and retention. The researcher may delimit the participant sample to tenured teachers who remained in teaching and tenured teachers who chose to leave teaching in a large urban district. The researcher then selects participants based on criteria that she or he imposes on the sample to form the participant group.

> A description of the participant sample is located in the methodology chapter.

Example 1

In the first example, the researcher uses the term participant sample to indicate that the size of the sample satisfied reliability requirements. The researcher in the second example describes the demographic composition of the participants in the researcher's study.

Participant Sample

> The participating schools included programs that only identified gifted students and those that provided the maximum number of services allowed in Missouri (Fink, 2006; Heppner & Heppner). By including all 291 school districts with gifted programs, the participant sample was of sufficient size to increase the reliability of the data collected (Gay & Airasian, 2003; Heppner & Heppner). (Christian, 2008, p. 64)

Example 2

Participant Sample

Participants: Composition of the Sample

> As is common in qualitative research, the required sample size was unknown in advance of the study. This decision was left to the discretion of the researcher, and it was guided by the following criteria (Lincoln & Guba, 1985): Exhaustion of information sources, saturation of categories (i.e., no further thematic differentiation), emergence of regularities, and overextension or redundancy of information. Based on these criteria, data were obtained from twenty-five participants. They were represented by the following sports: wresting (8), basketball (3), soccer (5), track and field (5), and football (4). The sample consisted of twenty-two males and three females. The mean age was 21.24 years (SD = 3.47). The mean duration

> of involvement in their respective sport was 10.86 years (SD = 3.72). Seven participants competed at the intercollegiate level. Six competed at the national level. Seven competed internationally, and five competed at the World Championship 1 Olympic level. (Roy, 2004, pp. 49–50)

Participant Sample Checklist

- ☐ The participant sample is the larger group from which the study's participants are drawn.
- ☐ The study's participants mirror the demographic make-up of the participant sample.
- ☐ The researcher describes the attributes of the participant sample and provides a rationale for the sample.
- ☐ The researcher may delimit (see *delimitations*) the participant sample.

PARTICIPANTS (also Human Subjects)

> A description of the participants or human subjects is located in the methodology chapter. See *human subjects* for description, definition, and checklist.

Example

In this example, the researcher describes the participants and the context from which the participants were recruited to participate in the study.

Participants

> The 10 participants in this study were students in Algebra II classes at the Duke University Talent Identification Program's Summer Studies Programs (TIP), which are intense three-week residential sessions that are designed to provide participants with the equivalent of a year-long high school course. TIP participants are generally highly motivated and mathematically gifted students who are seeking an opportunity to accelerate their educational experiences. To qualify for mathematics courses offered by the Talent Identification Program (TIP), seventh-grade academically

gifted students scored 570 or better on the mathematics section of the Scholastic Aptitude Test (SAT).

From a pool of 20 students who volunteered to participate in the study, 10 students were purposefully selected using a process described by Patton (2002) as maximum variation sampling, defined as the selection of a wide variety of cases to attain variation on dimensions of interest. The researcher used teacher input to select several students who seemed to master the material almost effortlessly, several students who were struggling, and several students between these extremes. This selection process was chosen in order to gain the greatest possible breadth of understanding of the common threads of student strategies and connection-making.

The 10 students who were interviewed as part of this study came from diverse backgrounds and ability levels compared to the other students in their TIP classes. An examination of the students' pretests indicated that these students did not possess conceptual knowledge of polynomials when they began the course. All of the students, with the exception of Jason and Michael, had completed Algebra I and Geometry prior to attending TIP. Jason and Michael had both completed Algebra I only. None of the students had taken Algebra II previously. In order to ensure confidentiality, all names used are pseudonyms. (Teachey, 2003, pp. 83–84)

PILOT TESTING

The researcher pilot tests or pilots his or her measures, protocols, and experimental processes prior to initiating the study with a pilot group. The pilot group mirrors the demographic make-up of the study's participants. In piloting the measures, protocols, or experimental processes, the researcher is careful to simulate the study's conditions. In doing so, she or he perfects the measures, protocols, or previously untested experimental processes. The researcher must have pilot group participants sign letters of consent. The consent forms are part of the Institutional Review Board (IRB) proposal sent to the IRB for study approval.

The researcher collects data from the piloting process and makes appropriate modifications to his or her measures, protocols, or experimental processes. The data gathered in the piloting process is not considered part of the study's data-gathering process. The researcher clearly describes the pilot group and any modifications made to the study's measures, protocols, and experimental processes (Hershey, Jacobs-Lawson, & Wilson, 2005). The researcher places the pilot testing material in the appendices of the dissertation.

> A description of pilot testing or piloting is located the methodology chapter.

Example

In this example, the researcher describes the purpose for pilot testing. The researcher also describes the protocols used in the pilot test.

Pilot Testing

> To assess the effectiveness of the attractiveness manipulation before beginning the study, I performed pilot testing with a convenience sample of 43 male university students enrolled in a Statistical Methods in Psychology course. Students received extra credit for participating. Each student anonymously and voluntarily viewed four still images of one of the female confederates, taken from the video segments, in either the attractive condition or the unattractive condition. . . . Pilot testing with the first five people who signed up for the study served as a rehearsal for the experimenter and elicited detailed feedback from those individuals about the procedures. The feedback that was provided confirmed that the non-alcoholic beer was a convincing placebo, the instructions were clear, the cover story was believable, and that the reasons for the design of the study were understood and appreciated. I made some slight changes to the script to enhance the plausibility of the cover story before full data collection began; for example, I told participants that the female participant was participating in a room on another hallway because one pilot-testing participant thought it was odd that he did not see her in the hallway while waiting for the study to begin. I also added a line asking participants not to try to gesture or communicate with the other participant by webcam because it became obvious that students would try to communicate without such an instruction. (Rider, 2006, pp. 51–52)

Pilot Testing Checklist

- ☐ The measures, protocols, or experimental processes used in the study are piloted prior to their use.
- ☐ Pilot group participants mirror the participants selected for the study.
- ☐ Any modifications to measures, protocols, or experimental processes are fully described.
- ☐ Pilot group participants sign letters of consent approved by the IRB prior to their participation in the pilot study.
- ☐ The researcher places the pilot testing material in the appendices of the dissertation.

POPULATION

The population is the group from which a sample is drawn (see sample for a definition). In quantitative research, the population of a study represents the group that the researcher has as the object of his or her study; it is the group toward whom the researcher generalizes his or her findings and results (Trochim, 2006). The researcher describes the decision for defining the population and the size of the population from which she or he selected the sample.

> A description of the population is located in the methodology chapter.

Example

In this example, the researcher describes the population for the study and how the sample was drawn from the population.

Population

Study Population

The population of this study consists of all university-based educational administration preparation programs in the United States; according to Lane (2002) and McLeod (2002), there are approximately 525 such pro-

> grams (Appendix J). Of the 525 programs, 138 were not included due to lack of sufficient contact information (i.e., incorrect or no e-mail address available to researcher), leaving a sample population of 387 programs. (Witt, 2003, p. 37)

Population Checklist

- ☐ Ensure that the population is fully described.
- ☐ Ensure that the decision to define the population is straightforward.
- ☐ Ensure that the population is broad enough to make generalizations.
- ☐ Ensure that the sample is drawn from the population.

PRESENTATION AND ANALYSIS OF THE DATA (see Analysis)

PROBLEM STATEMENT

The problem statement is the heart of the dissertation. The research questions and hypotheses, methodology, theoretical perspectives, and literature review all flow from the problem statement. The researcher describes the problem statement by framing the issue that she or he plans to study, thus creating a case that the issue is important to study. The problem statement leads to a succinct closing statement of the problem that clearly presents an interrogative sentence (question) seeking to determine the relationship between two or more variables. Clark, Guba, and Smith state:

> A problem is a situation resulting from the interaction or juxtaposition of two or more factors (e g., givens, constraints, conditions, desires, etc.) which yields (1) a perplexing or enigmatic state, (2) an undesirable consequence, or (3) a conflict which renders the choice from among alternative courses of action moot. (1977, p. 7)

A full presentation of the problem statement is located in the introductory chapter.

Example

In this example, the researcher presented a lengthy rationale for the problem statement. At the conclusion of the rationale, the researcher presented a succinct problem statement.

Problem Statement

> Therefore, the problem addressed in this study was: from the perspective of the faculty members, faculty developers, trainers, and policy makers, were the ET faculty development activities effective; what are the elements of their effectiveness; and what were their impacts on the participants' profession and practices, students' learning, and the organization's development? (Al-Washahi, 2007, p. 23)

Problem Statement Checklist

- ☐ The researcher presents a clear rationale for the problem.
- ☐ The problem statement identifies the variables that are being studied.
- ☐ The problem statement juxtaposes the variables.
- ☐ The problem statement uses an interrogative statement to express the problem.

PROCEDURES (also Data Collection)

In Chapter 3, the researcher describes (1) the study's data collection procedures, (2) the connection between the data collection procedures and the research questions, and (3) implementation of the data collection procedures based on the study's protocol. The researcher may include a copy of the study's manual of operations or standard operating procedures document in the appendices. The researcher describes the study's procedures: (1) how she or he recruited participants, (2) the steps taken to gain informed consent, (3) the care taken to protect participants, (4) protocols for collecting data, (5) feedback mechanisms for the participants, (6) protection of the data, and (7) documentation of study data. The researcher also describes his or her efforts to maintain consistency in collecting data to increase the data's reliability (National Institute of Child Health and Human Development, 2008). A detailed trail of how procedures were consistently applied throughout the study is summarized in the methodology chapter and fully presented in the appendices. Depending on the length, some of the study's data collection procedures may be developed as appendices.

> A description of the research study's data collection procedures is located in the methodology chapter.

Example

The term *procedure* applies to several aspects of study reported in the dissertation. The term may apply to data analysis (see the example in procedures for data analysis), the protocols in a quasi-experimental study, or, as in this example, data collection procedures. The central point in all cases when reporting procedures is to report the procedures with precision so the reader has sufficient information to replicate the study, as the researcher did in the following example.

Data Collection Procedures

> Initially, the study collected data from four groups of research participants: the 2006 GSW Placement Program Participants, the 2006 GSW Instructor Participants, the 2006 BGSU Student Participants, and Former and Current GSW Instructors. (Refer to Chapter Three, "Methodology," pp. 71-82, for a detailed summary and theoretical rationale of the research instruments created to triangulate data from these participants.) In synopsis, various instruments and procedures were utilized to collect data from the Placement Program Participants: audio taped pair evaluation sessions; videotaped placement training sessions and audio taped norming sessions; first and second individual interviews; first and second interviews with paired evaluators; first and second group interviews; and program documents. Moreover, one focus group interview was conducted with 2006 GSW Instructor participants; fifty sample essays were collected from 2006 BGSU student participants; and e-mail questionnaires were collected from former and current GSW instructors. (Refer to "Appendix H: Consent Forms and Scripts for the Study," pp. 671–703, for the final HSRB approved script for each instrument.) (Stalions, 2007, p. 87)

Procedures Checklist

- ☐ The study's data collection procedures are detailed.
- ☐ The study's data collection procedures may be referenced in the appendices.
- ☐ A detailed trail of how procedures were consistently applied throughout the study is summarized in the methodology chapter and fully presented in the appendices.

PROCEDURES FOR DATA ANALYSIS

The researcher describes the procedures used for data analysis to allow others to replicate the study. She or he provides sufficient information to demonstrate that the data analysis procedures flow from the research design, research questions, and hypotheses, and theoretical perspectives guiding the study. The researcher is transparent in asserting the assumptions in the application of statistics, data properties, and choosing levels of significance. If the study has a small number of participants, the researcher describes how statistical power issues were resolved. In qualitative research, the researcher describes the procedures to ensure the trustworthiness of the data, validity of the data, and reduction of bias (McGaghie & Crandall, 2001).

> A description of the data analysis procedures is located in the methodology chapter.

Example

In this example, the researcher describes the qualitative data analysis procedures used in the study.

Data Analysis Procedures

Consistent with qualitative research, data collection and analysis were conducted simultaneously. Merriam (1998) affirmed the interactive nature of data collection, analysis, and reporting. A qualitative design is emergent. The researcher usually does not know ahead of time every person who might be interviewed, all questions that might be asked, or where to look next unless data are analyzed as they are being collected (Merriam, 1998).

Data were analyzed working inductively from the particulars to more general perspectives to derive themes of categories (Creswell, 1998). One way to conduct an inductive analysis of qualitative data is the constant comparative method (Glaser & Strauss, 1967; Lincoln & Guba, 1985). In the constant comparative method each new category of meaning selected for analysis is compared with all other categories of meaning and grouped (Maykut & Morehouse, 1994). Because it is a continual, evolving process, the constant comparative method was chosen as the process for refining categories and deriving themes for this study. (Sheehy, 2007, pp. 90–91)

Data Analysis Procedures Checklist

- ☐ The study's data analysis procedures are detailed to provide replication of the study.
- ☐ The study's data analysis procedures are accurate, substantive, and follow established data analysis strategies, allowing the reader to trust the analysis and the findings and results emerging from the analysis.

PROCEDURES TO PROTECT HUMAN SUBJECTS/PARTICIPANTS (see Procedures and Institutional Review Board)

PURPOSE OF THE STUDY/PURPOSE STATEMENT

The purpose of the study is a succinct restatement of the problem statement. The purpose of the study offers a precise summation of the study (Calabrese, 2006). The purpose of the study statement also includes the variables studied and the primary unit of analysis.

> A description of the purpose of the study is located in the introductory chapter, is repeated in the methodology chapter, and is restated verbatim in the findings and results chapters.

Example

In this example, the researcher begins the purpose statement with a succinct statement of purpose. She or he then expands her or his description and provides a rationale for the purpose of the study.

Purpose of the Study

> The purpose of the present study was to examine the verbal social communication patterns of children with special needs, such as statements of helping, rejection, competition, self-worth, consideration, intrusiveness, and persuasiveness. Specifically, the researcher investigated the patterns of verbal social communication displayed by children, ages 5–9, during a cooperative group art project. This population was chosen because children with special needs are often the most challenging to teach (Green, 1999). Specifically, these children utilize different communication techniques and verbal messages than children without these special needs (Speckman, 1981). However, by gaining an understanding of their social relationships and communicative strategies, educators may gain insight as to how to teach these children. (Conde, 2006, p. 43)

Purpose of the Study Checklist

- ☐ Ensure that the purpose of the study contains the variables that were studied.
- ☐ Ensure that the purpose of the study succinctly identifies the intent of inquiry.
- ☐ Ensure that the purpose of the study contains the study's unit of analysis.

Q

QUALITATIVE ANALYSIS (see Analysis [Qualitative])

QUANTITATIVE ANALYSIS (see Analysis [Quantitative])

QUESTIONS LEFT UNANSWERED (see Implications for Future Research)

R

RATIONALE FOR DATA PRESENTATION AND ANALYSIS (see Analysis [Qualitative] and Analysis [Quantitative])

RATIONALE FOR THE DESIGN (see Research Design)

RATIONALE FOR THE STUDY (see Need for the Study)

RECOMMENDATIONS FOR FURTHER STUDY (see Implications for Future Research)

RECOMMENDATIONS FOR FUTURE RESEARCH (see Implications for Future Research)

RECOMMENDATIONS

An educational researcher makes recommendations from his or her study to advance the work of practitioners. The recommendations are specific and target acts of practice with suggested modifications, new models, action plans, or different points of view. The recommendations flow from the findings and results; they are not written as juxtaposed to current practices. Instead, they are offered as the researcher's speculation as to how his or her research can constructively alter current practices yielding enhanced outcomes.

> A full description of the recommendations is located in the discussion chapter.

Example

In this example, the researcher provides recommendations for three separate groups: Two groups are related to practice and the third group is for future research. The example presents the recommendations to one group related to practice. Place recommendations in the discussion chapter.

Recommendations

This section will present the recommendations of the researcher, divided into three groups, based on the findings of this study.

For Policy-Makers

Considering the limitation of this study, and its primary focus on the practice of citizenship education from the teachers' perspectives in the three selected countries, the findings suggest some policy questions that need to be addressed and evaluated by education policy makers in these countries:

1. Is there a need to develop training and professional development programs for teachers, particularly with the introduction or modification of a school subject such as civics?

2. Is there a need to offer teachers more opportunities to be involved in designing a civics curriculum, which might be accomplished by delegating the development of a curriculum or a part of it to local educational authorities?

3. Is there a need to improve the quality of materials and textbooks used in civics instruction, which should facilitate the adoption of national standards and guidelines? (Zaman, 2006, p. 83)

Recommendations Checklist

- ☐ The recommendations link the findings and results to practice.
- ☐ The recommendations are consistent with the researcher's belief of how practice is conducted.
- ☐ The recommendations are speculative based on the researcher's theory of practice.
- ☐ The recommendations are placed in the discussion chapter.

REFERENCES

The references section in the dissertation lists the works cited within the dissertation. The reference section in the dissertation (1) only cites works that were used in the dissertation, (2) provides enough information for the reader to retrieve the source document, (3) ensures that entries are accurate and complete (American Psychological Association, 2001), and (4) conforms to the department or graduate school stylistic policy.

The references are located at the end of the traditional dissertation.

References Checklist

- ☐ Each source cited in the dissertation is also referenced in the list of references in the references section.
- ☐ Each reference is accurate.
- ☐ Each reference provides sufficient information for retrieval.
- ☐ The format of the references section follows department or graduate school guidelines.

RELATIONSHIP OF RESEARCH TO THEORY, RESEARCH, AND PRACTICE

The researcher describes the study's findings and results in relationship to existing theory, empirical research, and current practice. She or he identifies how the findings and results inform, advance, or contradict theory, empirical research, and current practice. If the researcher's findings and results inform or advance theory, research, or practice, she or he begins with summative statements of theory, research, and practice, and demonstrates how his or her research provides an alternative view of how inquiry might occur in these areas.

The researcher does not make universal claims; instead, she or he frames the narrative in a speculative framework that encourages further inquiry. If the researcher's findings and results contradict existing theory, research, or practice, she or he offers an alternative explanation. The researcher's work does not condemn the previous line of inquiry; instead, it suggests that her or his work opens new lines of inquiry.

> A description of the relationship of research to theory, research, and practice is located in the discussion chapter.

Example

In this example, the researcher frames the relationship of research conducted in the study to theory and application.

Relationship of Research to Theory

Contribution of Research to Theory and Application

The contribution of this research to the integrative communication theory brings greater understanding to the process of adaptation. This particular cohort was interested in the integration mode (Berry, 1990). They wanted to maintain their own Indian cultural integrity, but also develop relations with other group members. However, this cohort also showed signs of the separation mode (Berry, 1990). They preferred to socialize among themselves rather than the dominant culture. In fact, they used media (i.e. American television) to help them integrate in the work place, which is why this study can be linked to the uses and gratifications theoretical perspective. This cohort was definitely not interested in assimilating, that is, losing their original cultural identity and only forming relations with members of the dominant culture (Berry, 1990). This cohort was also not interested in being marginalized, that is, neither maintaining their cultural identity nor forming relations with other group members in the society (Berry, 1991).

These Asian Indians functioned at both the group level and individual level of acculturation (Berry, 1990). Forming Indian associations in their new host country so all members of the Asian Indian community could come together and participate in cultural activities was an example of the group level of acculturation. At the individual level of acculturation, these Asian Indians' behavior and attitude changed as they saw the value of getting to know their work colleagues on a non-work related level. (Somani, 2008, pp. 222–223)

Relationship of Research to Theory, Research, and Practice Checklist

- ☐ Identify the linkage of the findings and results to relevant theory, research, and practice.
- ☐ Provide a rationale that describes how the findings inform, advance, or contradict relevant theory, research, and practice.

RELIABILITY (also Reliability Analyses)

The researcher describes how she or he ensured the reliability of the study. This description assures the reader that the study's results are consistent for the same population using the same measure or different forms of the same measure (Crocker, 2006). In describing the steps taken to ensure reliability, the researcher provides sufficient information to make an informed decision that the research design and data collection methods are trustworthy. The researcher's description of the reliability of the study allows the reader to consider either the generalizability or transferability of the study (Howell, et al., 2005). In quantitative research, the researcher provides information related to the way she or he determined instrument reliability by reporting the correlation coefficient for internal consistency, split-half reliability, test-retest reliability, or inter-rater reliability (Garson, n.d.).

> A description of the research study's reliability is located in the methodology chapter.

Example

In this example, the researcher presents reliability for the survey instrument used in this study. The researcher also presents validity data in this paragraph.

Reliability

> Reliability and validity data for the SSS were analyzed by the authors of the survey instrument (Saunders, Cooper, Winston, & Chernow, 2000) and are presented below. The internal consistency reliability of the SSS was calculated by use of a Cronbach's alpha coefficient. The SSS had an alpha coefficient of .94. The range of item-total correlation was .44 to .75 (Saunders, Cooper, Winston, & Chernow, 2000, p. 185). Validity of the SSS was estimated by correlating scores on the SSS with scores on the Index of Occupational Reaction (IOR), (Smith, 1976) and the Organizational Commitment Questionnaire (OCQ), (Porter & Smith, 1970). "The Pearson product-moment correlation between the IOR and SSS was .91 ($n = 275$, $p < .001$) and between the OCQ and SSS was .64 ($n = 275$, $p < .001$)," (Saunders, Cooper, Winston & Chernow, 2000). (Tull, 2004, p. 31)

Reliability Checklist

- ☐ The description of the study's reliability informs the reader that the results are replicable.
- ☐ The reliability of the study provides sufficient information to allow the reader to make an informed decision related to the study's generalizability or transferability.
- ☐ The description of the reliability provides sufficient information to allow the reader to trust the results of the study.
- ☐ The researcher provides the correlation coefficients for reliability and the means by which they were derived.

RELIABILITY ANALYSES (see Reliability)

RESEARCH CONTEXT (see Context of the Study)

RESEARCH DESIGN (also Design of the Study and Rationale for the Design)

The researcher describes the research design used for the study—the way she or he plans to conduct the study. She or he describes the research design to speak to the study's coherence demonstrating that parts of the study cohesively work together to address the research questions (Neto-Sydenstricker, 1997; Trochim, 2006). Yin (2003) identifies five aspects of a quality research design: (1) the research questions; (2) the study's propositions (assumptions); (3) the study's unit of analysis or sample; (4) the rationale for linking data to the study's propositions; and (5) the criteria the researcher used for explaining the findings and results. A sound and well-communicated research design provides confidence to the reader for trusting the researcher's results.

> A complete description of the research design is located in the methodology chapter.

Example 1

In this example, the researcher describes the study's research design. The researcher describes a mixed methodology research design to collect data.

Research Design

This study was a descriptive survey. It used multiple or mixed methodologies, including questionnaires and interviews. The research question being answered determined the type of methodology used. The importance of descriptive research is posited by Gall, Borg, and Gall (1996) who stated "unless researchers first generate an accurate description of an educational phenomenon as it exists, they lack a firm basis for explaining or changing it" (p. 374). Mixed methods studies are "those that combine the qualitative and quantitative approaches into the research methodology of a single study or multi-phased study" (Tashakkori & Teddlie, 1998, p. 17–18). Richardson (2003), in a study to understand teacher participants' perceptions of their professional responsibility, used a combined quantitative and qualitative method. The qualitative data revealed insightful data from write-in items included in the questionnaire for coding and constant comparative analysis as described by Glaser and Strauss (1967). Constant comparative analysis involves examining data, grouping them according to themes, and generating new theory or concepts that emerge from the data. Pritchard and Marshall (2002) used the qualitative procedure of constant comparative analysis and quantitative analyses in their study of healthy and unhealthy school districts, which allowed for in-depth analysis that one method by itself, could not achieve. (Johnson, 2004, p. 44)

Example 2

In this example, the researcher begins this chapter by identifying the research design. The researcher then presents a rationale on the strengths and weaknesses of the research design.

Research Design

This chapter presents the development of an appropriate research design and methodology to address the research questions in the field of study.

The field of study in this inquiry focuses on the perspectives of educational developers supporting the conduct of assessment online, so there was a strong initial orientation to adopt a qualitative rather than a quantitative paradigm because perspectives are best expressed in the individual voices of educational developers; furthermore, there are significant considerations around the contextual differences in Australian universities. A range of possible methodologies was systematically considered before a decision was made to adopt a multiple-case study approach.

Reeves (2003a) has identified flaws in research studies in e-learning, including lack of linkages to theoretical foundations, inadequate literature reviews, poor sample sizes, and meaningless discussion of results; Reeves (2002) has also specifically argued the case for better research on the demands of online teaching on tertiary staff. Coomey and Stephenson (2001, p. 38) recognize shortcomings in the size of samples in e-learning programs, often less than fifteen learners with the quality of programs also indeterminate. In reviewing research in the area of ICT and learning and teaching, Conole (2004) acknowledges that much of the current research has been criticized for being anecdotal and lacking in theoretical underpinnings; furthermore, there is a need for explicit models of course development for e-learning and assessment, as well as an understanding of the way technology impinges on both organizational structures and individual teaching staff within institutions.

> Gunawardena (2001) concludes that the complexities of online learning call for the use of multiple methods and multiple sources of data to understand group and individual perspectives. Table 3.2 provides an overview of the process that led to the decision to adopt a multiple case study approach and indicates some of the literature that was influential in that choice. (Donnan, 2007, pp. 61–63)

Research Design Checklist

- ☐ Each component of the study is tied to the research design.
- ☐ The type of study (e.g., qualitative, quantitative, mixed methods) is indicated in the research design.
- ☐ The description of the research design provides logic for linking together all aspects of the study.

RESEARCH GOALS

The empirical research reported in the dissertation is guided by research objectives and research goals. The researcher understands that goals for the study come from reflective questions generated by the study's problem statement. The researcher asks two questions: (1) What do I want to accomplish by this research, and (2) What are the outcomes I expect from this research study? The researcher's answers have a direct link to the problem statement and the research questions. A research goal may be to generate new theory linked directly to practice, development (as in the case of the following example), or to further a line of inquiry.

> A complete description of research goals is located in the methodology chapter.

Example

Some researchers term research goals objectives. In this example, the researcher provides an introduction to the study's research goals and then delineates the study's two primary research goals.

Research Goals

Different goals or purposes of research call for different research methods (Reeves & Hedberg, 2003). Clarifying the research goals of the study helps determine the appropriate methodology.

Reeves and Hedberg (2003) identify six major types of research goals in the field of educational technology: theoretical goals, predictive goals, interpretivist goals, postmodern goals, development goals, and action goals. Theory construction is the major activity for researchers with theoretical goals, whereas predictive goals aim to determine or predict the effects of technological innovations under controlled conditions. Studies with interpretivist goals portray education-related phenomena, and researchers with postmodern goals are interested in examining assumptions and "revealing hidden agendas and/or empowering disenfranchised minorities" (Reeves & Hedberg, 2003, p. 267). Development goals and action goals are at the practice end of the "theory versus practice" continuum. Development goals focus on developing creative approaches to problem solving and at the same time generating design principles. Action goals are similar to development goals, but they have less emphasis on theory and principle development. Action goals aim to solve "a particular problem in a specific place within a relatively short timeframe" (Reeves & Hedberg, 2003, p. 268).

The goals of the study are twofold: (a) to identify faculty perceptions of a case library so as to support decision making with regard as to whether to adopt it as an online teaching resource, and (b) to provide design knowledge for developing this tool. These are development goals, which have the dual purposes of solving problems and constructing design principles (Reeves & Hedberg, 2003). Development goals can be achieved with development research (Reeves et al., 2004; Richey et al., 2003). (Ma, 2006)

Research Goals Checklist

- ☐ Each research goal has a direct link to the problem statement.
- ☐ Each research goal provides logic linking the projected outcomes of the study to a specific target.

RESEARCH HYPOTHESIS (see Hypotheses)

RESEARCH METHODS (see Methods)

RESEARCH PROCESS

Some dissertation advisors require advisees to define the research process. The researcher describes the research process as emanating from the research problem. The research process is composed of (1) research questions and hypotheses that specifically address the research problem, (2) theoretical perspectives or theoretical framework for inquiry into the research problem, (3) the study's unit of analysis, (4) a clear rationale that describes how data collected in the study addresses the research questions and hypotheses, (5) and the researcher's explanation for deriving findings (Yin, 2003). In many cases, the parts to the research process are disaggregated into separate sections in the introductory chapter of the dissertation.

> A description of the research process in located in the introductory chapter or the methodology chapter.

Research Process Checklist

- ☐ Describe research questions and hypotheses that specifically address the problem statement.
- ☐ Describe theoretical perspectives or theoretical framework for inquiry into the problem statement.
- ☐ Describe the study's unit of analysis.
- ☐ Explain the rationale that describes how data collected in the study addresses the research questions and hypotheses, and explanation for deriving findings.
- ☐ Present a logical sequence for the research process.
- ☐ Link all parts of the research process into a coherent whole.

RESEARCH QUESTIONS

The researcher links the research questions to the study's problem statement. The research questions, if answered, address the problem raised in the problem statement. Research questions typically begin with who, what, why, or how. A well-constructed research question contains three parts: the unit of analysis, an action or relational word, and the object of the action or relational word. The researcher understands that a well-constructed research question is singular in purpose—emphasizing specificity of action. There is one unit of analysis, one action, and one object of action.

> The research questions are located initially in the introductory chapter. They are repeated verbatim in the methodology chapter, and repeated verbatim in the results chapter.

Example

In this example, the researcher lists two research questions. Both questions begin with the interrogatory "what." Each research questions has the three parts mentioned in the previous definition.

Research Questions (Hodum, 2007, p. 29)

This study was designed to answer two primary questions:

1. What characteristics of a new-student orientation program are perceived to promote socialization?
2. What characteristics of a new-student orientation program are perceived to have an influence on student retention?

Research Questions Checklist

- ☐ Each research question addresses the problem introduced in the problem statement.
- ☐ Each research question is specific.
- ☐ Each research question contains three parts: the unit of analysis, an action word, and an object of the action word.
- ☐ Each research question typically begins with who, what, why, or how.

RESEARCH STRATEGY

The researcher identifies the research strategy in the study. In some cases, the researcher may have used multiple strategies. The researcher's research strategy frames research questions and hypotheses that address the study's problem statement. The research strategy defines the study's research needs by identifying the priorities to address the research questions and hypotheses. The researcher's research strategy provides a framework linking the goals of the research with the research design and methodologies best suited to address the research questions and hypotheses (U.S. Environmental Protection Agency, 2008).

> A description of the research strategy is located in the methodology chapter.

Example

In this example, the researcher indicates the research strategy for the study and provides a rationale for this strategy.

Research Strategy

> The intention in using this research technique was to take the cross-site themes that had emerged back to Roundtable members for verification, refinement, and further exploration. Fontana and Frey (Denzin & Lincoln, 1994a: 364–365) note that group interviews, as a qualitative research strategy, can be data-rich because they are recall aiding, cumulative, elaborative, and draw on group diversity. In addition they can be stimulating for participants, and they have the advantage of being inexpensive and flexible. The group interviews, conceived in terms of an explicit shared reflection between participants in the Western Melbourne Roundtable, were the final stage in checking the main themes emerging in the study. (Davies, 2005, p. 98)

Research Strategy Checklist

- ☐ The research strategy contains an explicit framework for the research.
- ☐ The research strategy identifies the linkage between the study's goals and the selected methodologies.

- ☐ The research strategy has a well-articulated rationale to address the focal point of inquiry.

RESEARCHER'S BACKGROUND FOR CONDUCTING THE STUDY

The researcher brings knowledge and experience to the research. The researcher's experiential background may include cultural, work, or personal experiences. From these experiences, the researcher develops tacit theories related to his or her experiences. These tacit theories allow the researcher to make sense of his or her environment or work. The researcher's experiential background is informed by his or her knowledge base. The knowledge base is the researcher's formal learning that interacts with informal learning. Out of this interaction, the researcher identifies a personal theory related to the focus of inquiry.

> In some dissertations, the researcher's background is a section in the conceptual framework in the literature review chapter. In other dissertations, it is presented in the methodology chapter.

Example

In this example, the researcher describes her background as part of the study's conceptual framework presented in the literature review chapter.

Researcher's Background

> The conceptual framework was composed of my experience, epistemology, theoretical perspectives, and assumptions. First, my experiences, which inform my beliefs and values, were partially responsible for formulating my conceptual framework. My experiences, beliefs, and values have continually generated moments in which I have been attracted to people who were interested in sharing or exploring personal distinct experiences considered both exceptionally challenging and rewarding—all of which I call peak experiences.
>
> My experience as a practicing educator, teacher, coach, and administrator, as well as my experience as a student, to include current graduate studies, informed my interests and research design. I believe people do

> their best and have much to offer by sharing their perspectives of peak experiences. I value my role as a leader and educator to provide people with generative occasions in which they can reflect on their practice to create desired scenarios. I have the following beliefs about people: They behave according to (a) how things appear, (b) how they see themselves, (c) how they view situations they confront, and (d) how they form the purposes they hold at the moment in which they act. I also believe to gain a clear view of teachers' peak experiences in a teaching and learning context requires a connection with those who can describe peak experiences. In my research, the claims, concerns, and issues of teachers served as the basis for determining what information was needed to fully capture the essence of peak experiences in a teaching and learning context. (Hummel, 2007, pp. 12–13)

Researcher Background for Conducting the Study Checklist

- ☐ The researcher describes personal experience that contributed to the theories related to the study.
- ☐ Describe the extent of the knowledge base (formal and informal) that leads to a perspective regarding the study.

RESULTS (also Chapter 4 and Findings)

The researcher reports the results of the study. Results answer the what? of the study. Reporting the results of the study are important for several reasons: (1) They add to the existing knowledge base, (2) they allow other researchers the opportunity to replicate their study, and (3) they improve educational practices (Marczyk, DeMatteo, & Festinger, 2005). The researcher is transparent when reporting the results of the study by reporting results that support or do not support his or her research questions and hypotheses (Moher, 2007). The results of the researcher's study are presented straightforwardly, using only the recorded facts from the study without interpretation.

Example

In this example, the researcher describes how he or she presents the results from his or her study in the results chapter.

Results

> This chapter presents findings of the relationship between perceived employment self-efficacy (along with other selected factors) and work-readiness. The sample for this study was taken from participants in the New Connections to Work (NCTW) job training program in the greater Atlanta area. Results are presented in two parts. First, a description of those participating in the study is discussed. Second, results pertaining to the three main research objectives are presented. (Deloatch-Anthony, 2005, p. 100)

Results Checklist

- ☐ The results of the study are tied to outcomes of specific research questions and hypotheses.
- ☐ The results are presented without interpretation.

RÉSUMÉ (see Vita/Vitae)

REVIEW CONCLUSIONS

The researcher provides review conclusions as a succinct summary of the study's conclusions drawn from a review of the relevant empirical research. This succinct summary that is presented in the review conclusions acts as an organizer for the discussion of the conclusions. The review conclusions section is an organizer for discussion of the researcher's review of the empirical research where the researcher discusses findings emanating from a critical analysis of the relevant research.

> A description of the review conclusions is located in the literature review chapter.

Example

In this example, the researcher presents review conclusions in the discussion chapter of the dissertation. The review conclusions serve as an organizer for the researcher's discussion of conclusions drawn from a review of the relevant empirical research.

Review Conclusions

The literature has revealed the following conclusions:

1. Researchers tend to take a linear or unidimensional approach when investigating the links between school leadership/culture and effectiveness.
2. A unidimensional approach has a tendency to collapse or mask the complexity of dynamic organizational systems.
3. A multidimensional approach to school leadership/culture and effectiveness provides different perspectives coordinating around deeper, larger conceptual problems.
4. There is no synthesized definition of the multidimensional aspects of CLC from the literature.
5. The connection between CLC and school effectiveness are obscure, at best.
6. A conceptual model of the interrelationships of the multidimensional aspects of CLC and how it impacts school effectiveness is nonexistent.
7. Designing and undertaking a multidimensional investigation into any existing links between school leadership/culture and effectiveness could have a significant impact on the theoretical and practical knowledge that would be of a direct benefit to both researchers and practitioners. (Adams, 2007, p. 69)

Review Conclusions Checklist

- ☐ Succinctly summarize the study's conclusions.
- ☐ Use the review conclusions as an organizer for discussing the conclusions.
- ☐ Succinctly summarize the primary themes, trends, and conclusions drawn from the literature review in the review conclusions section in the literature review chapter.

ROLE OF THE RESEARCHER

The researcher fully discloses his or her role as researcher in the study in the dissertation. The researcher identifies any potential role conflicts that potentially affect the research setting (Kitchener, 2000). In many cases, the researcher conducts the research in a setting where she or he is employed. In these cases, the researcher discloses the potential effect of power relationships, bias, role expectations of the participants for the researcher, and the precautions she or he took to minimize the effect of the researcher's role on the conduct of the study or its outcomes (Kimmel, 1988). In qualitative research, the researcher describes her or his role as participant-observer, facilitator, interviewer, or other role. She or he indicates how she or he took care not to impose a bias on the study. In quantitative research, the researcher describes how she or he maintained neutrality and maximized the study's validity.

A description of the role of the researcher is located in the methodology chapter.

Example

In this example, the researcher describes the role of researcher in this study using the personal pronoun my. (Check with your department and university concerning the use of personal pronouns when writing your dissertation. It is common practice at most universities.) The researcher then describes all aspects of involvement in conducting the research.

Role of the Researcher

My Role

Van Manen (1997) identified the role of the researcher as one of collaborator in the process of reflecting on a participant's experience. I served as a data collection tool because I entered the lives of the participants in this qualitative investigation (Marshall & Rossman, 1999; Miles & Huberman, 1994). I used audiotape, pen, and paper to capture data. Each session was audio taped and I made relevant notes on both lined paper and the interview guide sheet as the session progressed.

I already had familiarity with the participants because of having taught them or having directed their teacher education program. Because of the time frame of this engagement with many types of interaction, a certain level of trust existed already. To promote continued trust, I was very open about the nature and purpose of the study, time requirements, use and storage of data, anonymity, and participant verification of data. I informed and gave participants the opportunity to verify the accuracy of the transcription when all three interviews were completed. I mailed the three completed transcriptions to participants with a letter asking for review and clarification if needed. I followed up with a phone call after one week to ascertain any need for clarification or revision. Further, I interviewed participants in their natural environment or an environment of their choosing that provided seclusion and freedom from interruptions (Van Manen, 1997). Interviews were held at school, home, or a private office free from distractions. I adhered to ethical standards for investigations involving human subjects as specified by the university. (White, 2002, p. 49)

Role of the Researcher Checklist

- ☐ The researcher fully discloses his or her role as researcher in the study.
- ☐ The description of the role of the researcher discloses any power relationships, bias, role expectations of the participants.
- ☐ The description of the role of the researcher includes precautions taken to minimize researcher bias related to the conduct of the study, data analysis, or study outcomes.

S

SAMPLE

A sample is a representation of a larger population the researcher chooses to study. The researcher describes the sample and the means she or he used to cull the sample as representative of a larger population. The researcher's description of the sample and its reliability as being representative of the whole advances the researcher's argument that the study's results are generalizable or transferable to the larger population from which the sample was drawn (O'Connor, 2006). She or he fully describes the population's demographic construction and criteria used to determine the sample size as well as criteria for the make-up of the sample.

The description of the sample is located in the methodology chapter.

Example

In this example, the researcher describes the sample as drawn from the representative population. The researcher also provides the rationale for participant selection into the sample.

Sample

Participants

Stake insists, "Case study research is not sampling research" (1995, p. 4). He continues suggesting that case study is more concerned with representation, albeit the smaller the sample the greater the difficulty to defend the representation (p. 4). He urges, "Balance and variety are important;

> opportunity to learn is of primary importance" (p. 5). Neither Stake (p. 5) nor Creswell (1998, p. 65) suggest a minimum number of participants for interviewing in a case study; however, this study sought to interview face to face as many of the 23 members of the cohort as possible. The 15 participants for the study were recruited from a cohort of 23 educational leaders who experienced the Courage to Teach for Educational Leaders (Courage to Lead [CTL]) program, which consisted of a five retreat series during the years 2002–2004. (Henderson, 2007, pp. 75–76)

Sample Checklist

- ☐ The sample is fully described.
- ☐ The population from which the sample was selected is fully described to the reader.
- ☐ The process for selecting the sample size as well as the composition of the sample is fully described.

SAMPLE SIZE

The researcher selects the size of the sample based on the goals of the study. The researcher demonstrates that the sample size was sufficient to address the research questions and hypotheses. A table is placed in the methodology chapter to represent a snapshot of the sample size. In quantitative research designs, the sample size is sufficient to yield statistical significance and allows the researcher to generalize his or her results (Lenth, 2001). In qualitative research designs, Merriam states, "It always depends on the questions being asked, the data being gathered, the analysis in progress, the resources to support the study" (2001, p. 64).

> The description of the sample size is located in the methodology chapter.

Example

In this example, the researcher presents how the sample size was drawn. The researcher presents a rationale for the choice of sample size.

Sample Size

Quantitative Research Sample

A cluster sample of students was drawn from students enrolled in courses that were identified by the LSU Office of Budget and Planning as having an enrollment of TOPS recipients that was greater than 75% during the 2003 Fall Semester. A listing of all courses with an enrollment of 75% or more of TOPS recipients was requested in conjunction with the initial request for a list of all TOPS recipients (see Appendix D). Class sizes ranged from one to 454 and the estimated average class size was thirty. These numbers were approximate because when the list of classes was produced, the last day to drop without receiving a grade of "W" had not passed.

A 95% confidence level was selected to help ensure that significant research findings would be true results and not sampling errors. A sample of 300 or more TOPS recipients was needed to ensure the 95% confidence level (Gall, Borg, & Gall, 1996). The 12,790 students who were currently on TOPS in 2003 composed approximately 42.6 % of the entire student body; therefore, 500 students were surveyed to increase the probability that the sample would meet or exceed the number of TOPS recipients needed. Demographic and educational experience data was collected from all 500 students in the sample. Because of the large population size, and the limitations presented through the process of acquiring access to the data, cluster sampling was used to distribute the sample more evenly over the available population to ensure more accurate results (Gall, Borg, & Gall, 1996). A random number between one and six was generated using SPSS. Students enrolled in the course that corresponded to the random number selected were included in the sample until the desired sample size of 500 was reached. The random selection process resulted in thirty-two classes that contained a 75% or greater student enrollment that were TOPS recipients. Although thirty-two classes were identified, access was only granted to the fifteen courses identified in Table 3.3. (Smothers, 2004, p. 52)

Sample Size Checklist

- ☐ The sample size is fully described.
- ☐ A table is placed in the methodology chapter to represent a snapshot of the sample size.

- ☐ Describe the power of the sample size in a quantitative study.
- ☐ Provide a rationale for the selection of the sample size in a qualitative study.

SIGNIFICANCE (see Significance of the Study)

SIGNIFICANCE OF THE STUDY

The researcher describes how the study (1) contributes to existing research, (2) benefits participants, (3) contributes to practice, and (4) generates new theory. If the significance of the study is presented in the dissertation proposal, the researcher is speculative, theorizing his or her contributions in these four areas. Once the study is completed, the researcher no longer speculates. She or he uses the findings of the study to describe the study's significance. She or he supports all claims with documentation from empirical research substantiated by the findings.

> The description of the significance of the study is located in the introductory chapter. It may also be located or expanded in the discussion chapter.

Example

In this example, the researcher presents a rationale for the study's significance based on the lack of empirical research in the researcher's line of inquiry. After the rationale for the study's significance, the researcher describes how the study will contribute to creating new knowledge and theory.

Significance of the Study

No studies were found that describe analytically the use of portfolios as a summative evaluation in programs preparing educational leaders, nor were any studies found that describe the implementation process, and perceptions and concerns of those carrying out the innovation. Therefore, the educational significance of this study is to synthesize and expand the knowledge base and to advance the existing body of knowledge in the field of portfolio assessment in educational leadership preparation programs at the master's degree level. (Vyortkina, 2003, p. 4)

Significance of the Study Checklist

- ☐ The significance of the study addresses how the study contributes to existing research, benefits participants, contributes to practice, and generates new theory.
- ☐ The significance of the study is supported by empirical research and the study's findings.

SOURCES OF EVIDENCE (see Data Sources)

STATEMENT OF THE PROBLEM (see Problem Statement)

STATISTICAL METHODS

The researcher recognizes that the statistical data analysis is present and substantive in reporting his or her original research. The statistical analysis is presented logically and coherently regarding the veracity of the analysis and findings and results derived from the analysis. The researcher describes the statistical methods she or he used by providing sufficient detail. The researcher uses care to demonstrate that she or he understands the statistical method and the method's purpose (Curran-Everett & Benos, 2004). The researcher presents the analysis from each statistical method with proper statistical notations (using tables where appropriate).

> A description of the statistical methods is located in the methodology chapter.

Example

In this example, the researcher provides a comprehensive description of the statistical methods used to analyze data collected in the study.

Statistical Methods

> Data collection from the survey was analyzed using the Statistical Package for Social Science (SPSS). This is a computer program that can provide both descriptive and inferential statistics. Descriptive summary statistics, including the number of responses for each variable, as well as the mean and standard deviation, was part of the initial analyses. After the initial analyses were conducted, data was analyzed to address each of the six research questions posed in the study.
>
> The Pearson Product-Moment, and two-way analysis of variance (ANOVA), were used to examine the research questions and six hypotheses to determine the relationships between the dependent and independent variables. With the number of analyses conducted on the six research questions, there were some concerns regarding the family-wise error rate. According to Tate (1998, p. 124), "the inflation of error rate can become quite serious as the size of the family rate increases." Instead of the usual alpha level of a = .05 that is recommended for educational research, the decision was made to control the family-wise error rate and to set a more rigorous level of significance for alpha (a = .01). (Duncon, 2004, pp. 82–83)

Statistical Methods Checklist

- ☐ The statistical methods are presented with analysis using appropriate statistical notations.
- ☐ The statistical methods for data analysis are supported by established statistical software packages such as SPSS.
- ☐ The statistical methods used for data analysis are the appropriate statistical methods to analyze the study's data.

STRUCTURE OF THE RESEARCH REPORT

Some dissertation advisers require their advisees to provide an introductory section detailing the structure of their dissertation. This section is titled Structure of the Research Report and provides an overview of the organization of the dissertation and the research conducted by the researcher. Most research reports follow a similar structure: introduction, review of relevant research, methodology, presentation of results, and discussion. In essence, they reflect the five chapters of the traditional dissertation.

A description of the structure of the research report is located in the introductory chapter.

Example

In this example, the researcher presents a succinct summary of the dissertation's structure. In many dissertations, this is commonly called the summary and is traditionally placed at the conclusion of the introductory chapter. In this format, it is placed at the introduction to the chapter.

> ***Structure of the Research Report***
>
> The structure of the research report is as follows: Chapter I outlines the literature on resiliency, leadership, and student autonomy. Chapter II outlines the study. It states the purpose of the study, provides definitions of terms, and explains the research design. Chapter II identifies the statement of the problem and the research questions. Chapter III contains the findings that describe the case study. The description is derived from data, document analysis, and the interviews, which were compiled and organized according to the research questions. Chapter IV outlines the summary, conclusions, implications for leadership practices, and implications for the development of resiliency in schools. (Cox, 2004, p. 50)

Structure of the Research Report Checklist

- ☐ Present a logical structure for reporting the research.
- ☐ Identify the introduction, review of relevant research, methodology, presentation of results, and discussion to the research report.

SUMMARY

The summary is an integral part of each chapter and many subsections located in the dissertation. The purpose of the summary is to provide clarity and closure of the subsections or chapter. Each chapter contains a summary of the chapter's contents addressing the chapter's salient points. Moreover, many subsections of each chapter contain a summary.

A summary, for example, should accompany the researcher's narrative of his or her theoretical perspectives. It follows the critical analysis of the empirical research. Sections that require summaries are methodology, data analysis, and each finding and result—especially in a qualitative study.

Example

In this example, the researcher provides a chapter summary. The researcher, earlier in the chapter, had a series of section summaries that are referenced in this example.

> *Summary*
>
> Chapter four provided a very in-depth description of each of the six cases in this study. The following information was provided for each case: a description of the demographic information of each district, the educational experiences of the person in charge of social studies curriculum, an overview of the content of the written curriculum, a summary of the constructs addressed in the curriculum, an overview of the contents of the student textbook, a summary of the constructs addressed in the textbook, a summary of the interview with the social studies coordinator, and finally a synthesis of the information gathered at the case.
>
> Chapter five will highlight the findings of this study in light of the research questions, provide recommendations for the future and outline potential future research topics. (Neville, 2006, p. 111)

Summary Checklist

- ☐ The summary synthesizes the salient points of the section or chapter.
- ☐ A summary section is used whenever the section is lengthy, with several important points.

SYNTHESIS OF FINDINGS

A synthesis of findings is commonly found in the literature review chapter. The researcher summarizes the primary findings, recommendations, lines of inquiry, and gaps in the research in this section. Emerging from the synthesis of findings is evidence for future research. If the researcher is synthesizing findings in the literature review, the evidence for future research supports the researcher's choice of problem to study. The researcher may add the findings from his or her study to the synthesis of findings in the literature review indicating how the findings advance or offer an alternative explanation or line of inquiry.

The synthesis of findings is located in the literature review chapter.

Example

In this example, the researcher succinctly describes the results of the review of the empirical research. The researcher disaggregates the findings by topics within the greater line of inquiry.

Synthesis of Findings

Findings

A summary of the findings for the research synthesis conducted on the effect of teacher certification on student achievement is presented in three sections that include (a) the meta-analysis population, (b) areas of achievement, and (c) meta-analysis findings.

The Meta-Analysis Population

Four different search strategies were used to obtain studies for the analysis and yielded a total of five studies. Three studies utilized either an individual level or class level of analysis and yielded twelve mean difference effect size estimates. Two studies utilized either a school or state level of analysis and yielded fifteen correlational effect size estimates. Therefore, the meta-analysis population was based on five studies that generated a total of twenty-seven effect size estimates.

Area of Achievement

Mathematics

The majority of findings favored the positive effect of certified teachers. The overall trend provides some support for the position that fully certified teachers yield higher achievement than less-than-fully certified teachers.

Science

> The overall trend provides no support for the position that fully certified teachers yield higher achievement in science than less-than-fully certified teachers.

Reading

> All the findings associated with reading favored the positive effect of fully certified teachers on student achievement. The overall trend supports the position that higher student achievement is associated with fully certified teachers. (Sparks, 2005, pp. 116–117)

Synthesis of Findings Checklist

- ☐ The synthesis of findings section describes the primary findings, recommendations, lines of inquiry, and gaps in the relevant research.
- ☐ The synthesis of findings section presents a logical presentation of the findings of existing relevant research.

T

TABLE OF CONTENTS

The table of contents provides a quick overview of the organization of the dissertation. The researcher organizes the table of contents using headers to identify chapters and sections of his or her dissertation. The table of contents follows the acknowledgments and abstract and precedes the list of tables and introductory chapter. In all cases, the researcher creates the headers throughout his or her dissertation based on graduate school and departmental norms. The headers allow software packages such as Microsoft Word to automatically create a table of contents. In general, three levels of headers are listed in the table of contents.

> The table of contents is located after the acknowledgments and abstract and precedes the list of tables and introductory chapter of the dissertation.

Example

The researcher should consult with his or her department and graduate school to determine the format for the table of contents. The use of headers in the software program Microsoft Word facilitates the automatic compilation and updating of a table of contents.

Table of Contents Checklist

☐ The table of contents meets the requirements of the graduate school and department.

- ☐ The table of contents has three levels of headers that allow for quick reference to specific sections of the dissertation.

TABLES

The researcher uses tables to summarize large amounts of data. Tables are clear, precise, generally presented in a logical format of rows and columns, and allow the reader to compare data by pre-specified categories. The tables are clear and provide the reader with understanding at a glance. Tables are supplemental to the text and allow the researcher to refer to the tables for supporting documentation to the researcher's narrative. The researcher only includes tables that are relevant and necessary and contribute to the understanding of the narrative. The researcher numbers all tables and begins numbering the first time the table is mentioned in the chapter. The researcher, for example, places several tables in Chapter 4. The first table is numbered as Table 4.1, followed by Table 4.2, 4.3, 4.4, and so on. The researcher gives each table a concise descriptive title (American Psychological Association, 2001).

> The tables can be located throughout the dissertation but generally are in the findings and results chapters.

Example

In this example, the researcher places tables in Chapter 2, reflecting search results, and in Chapter 4, reflecting findings.

List of Tables (Sheppard, 2007, p. xiii)

Tables Checklist

- ☐ Only relevant tables are placed in the dissertation.
- ☐ All tables are clear and unambiguous, offering ease of understanding and clarity.
- ☐ Tables summarize pertinent data that act as a supplement to the researcher's narrative.
- ☐ Tables are numbered and have a precise and descriptive table title.

THEORETICAL CONSTRUCTS

The researcher's theoretical constructs are based on the researcher's effort to explain an event, behavior, policy, or situation to others. Theoretical constructs are composed of ideas, theories, intuition, and propositions that the researcher has about an event, behavior, policy, or situation. The researcher's theoretical constructs are supported by the work of published theorists who influenced the researcher's line of inquiry. She or he describes how her or his theoretical constructs determine the research design and methodology that she or he chose to conduct the study.

> A description of the theoretical constructs is located in the literature review chapter.

Example

In this example, the researcher presented a lengthy discussion of the theory underlying the research undertaken. The researcher summarized the theoretical constructs in a paragraph following the lengthy discussion. The researcher identified these constructs in the introductory chapter.

Theoretical Constructs

> Scholars have demonstrated that the above noted theoretical constructs—neighborhood structural factors, strain, social capital, collective efficacy, and peer networks—are important for adolescent anti- and pro-social behaviors and decisions. However, empirical tests of these arguments have been for samples of youths in cities or samples of youths overall with no focus on geographic place as a relevant context. For example, data from a general, national sample of adolescents (the Panel Study of Income Dynamics) has shown that neighborhood structural characteristics (percentage of affluent families, female-headed families, and professional occupations) influence dropping out of school and teen childbearing (Brooks-Gunn et al. 1993). (Payne, 2007, p. 9)

Theoretical Constructs Checklist

- ☐ Theories used to explain or guide the study are identified.
- ☐ Theories are linked to the research study's methodology.

THEORETICAL FRAMEWORK

The researcher identifies and describes the theory that guides the study. In identifying the theory that guides the study, the researcher describes how she or he will make the theory operational. In some qualitative research, data are first collected and theory is generated from the data (see grounded theory). The researcher understands that theory is linked to practice and research. Theory provides the structure to examine practice and to inquire into practice. Theory is composed of a complex set of assumptions driven by observation, research, and intuition. As such, theory can be tested and generated. The researcher describes his or her theory in the form of a theoretical framework to guide the study. The researcher's choice of a well-developed theoretical perspective is grounded in the researcher's theory of the focus of inquiry. Yin (2003) suggests that this focus is essential for good research. The researcher makes his or her theory explicit and weaves it into the study's theoretical frameworks. In describing the theoretical frameworks, the researcher provides the theoretical and empirical antecedents to theoretical perspectives. In doing so, the researcher provides a rigorous defense for the choice of theory and theoretical perspectives that form his or her theoretical frameworks.

> A description of the theoretical framework is located in the literature review chapter.

Example

In this example, the researcher identifies one of the theories used to form the theoretical frameworks for the researcher's study. The researcher presents a brief introduction as to the selection of the theory.

Theoretical Frameworks

> Because of who I am as a Black Puerto Rican woman and because of the nature of my research topic, which is spirituality in early childhood education, one of the frameworks for the inquiry process was the Black feminist epistemology. Hill-Collins (2000) identifies the following as integral components or criteria of this framework: lived experience as a criterion for meaning, the use of dialogue, the ethic of personal accountability and the ethic of caring. When Black women make knowledge claims invoking the lived experience as a criterion for meaning, they are validating the personal knowledge and wisdom constructed from concrete experiences (Browning-Cole, 1993). Their lived experience gives them credibility (Ladson-Billings, 1997). In my experience as a teacher I shared with the participants some common challenges to nurture my own spirituality and that of the children within the school context. (Pedraza, 2006, p. 50)

Theoretical Framework Checklist

- ☐ The theoretical framework is composed of the researcher's theory and theoretical perspectives.
- ☐ The theoretical and empirical antecedents to the theoretical framework are evident.

THEORY

The researcher will use theory to guide his or her study. Theory, according to Kerlinger, "[is] a set of interrelated constructs (variables), definitions, and propositions that presents a systematic view of phenomena by specifying relations among variables with the purpose of explaining natural phenomena" (1979, p. 64). In some applications of a qualitative methodology, researchers use grounded theory. Grounded theory emerges from careful data analysis. In other forms of inquiry, the researcher initiates his or her study guided by theory. The researcher makes that theory explicit and supports its use with references to seminal works.

> A description of the theory that guides the research study is located in the introductory chapter. It is referred to as an explanation of the findings in the discussion chapter.

Example

In this example, the researcher presents the primary theory used in this study. The researcher describes the components of self-efficacy theory and provides numerous citations to support the use of the theory in the study.

Theory

Self-Efficacy Theory

Self-efficacy theory includes self-efficacy and outcome expectancy as major constructs (Bandura, 1997). Self-efficacy refers to beliefs about one's capabilities to learn or perform behaviors at designated levels (Bandura, 1986, 1997). To date, many studies have suggested that self-efficacy is a major determinant of activity choice, willingness to expend effort, performance and persistence in sport and physical activity (Feltz, 1982, 1984, 1988, 1992; Feltz & Magyar, 2006; Feltz & Mugno, 1983; McAuley, 1985, 1992; Moritz et al., 2000).

Outcome expectancy, on the other side, refers to a person's beliefs concerning the likely outcomes of a behavior (Bandura, 1997). In sport and physical activity, research has shown small to moderate associations between outcome expectancy and intentions among young adults (Bryan & Rocheleau, 2002; Dzewaltowski, 1989; Dzewaltowski et al., 1990; Trost et al., 2002). Although it was evident that the positive relationship between self-efficacy and outcome expectancy is promising (Corcoran & Rutledge, 1989; Kirsch, 1982; Williams et al., 2005), Bandura (1997) argued that the relationship between self-efficacy and outcome expectancy depends on how tightly contingencies between actions and outcomes are structured in a given domain of functioning. Apparently, the relationship between these two constructs in middle school physical education needs further investigation. (Gao, 2007, pp. 28–29)

Theory Checklist

- ☐ The theory is explicitly stated in the introductory chapter.
- ☐ Describe the theory's genesis, evolution, and relationship to the study's variables.
- ☐ The theory explains what was found in the study in the discussion chapter.

TITLE PAGE

The dissertation title page is subject to the guidelines of the researcher's graduate school, college, and department. In general, the dissertation's title page contains the following elements: Title, author, a statement indicating that the dissertation is in partial fulfillment of the type of degree (e.g., Doctor of Philosophy, Doctor of Education), degree concentration, university granting the degree, and year.

Example

The researcher should refer to his or her departmental and graduate school guidelines for the format of the title page.

Title Page Checklist

- ☐ The title page contains each of its specific elements.
- ☐ The title page conforms to the requirements of the researcher's graduate school and department.

TRIANGULATION OF FINDINGS

The researcher describes how collected data were triangulated to determine findings. The researcher identifies the forms of triangulation used: data, investigator, theoretical, or methodological. The researcher also describes the combinations of data collection methods that were used to triangulate the data. The researcher clearly indicates how triangulation of data ensures the confirmation and completeness of data. The researcher also describes how his or her application of triangulation confirmed the findings (Begley, 1996).

> A description of how triangulation was used in the research study is located in the methodology chapter.

Example

In this example, the researcher provides a comprehensive description of how data were triangulated.

Triangulation of Data

Triangulation describes the use of multiple data sources and/or research methods in a study. This apparent overlap by the qualitative researcher seeks to address threats to validity such as reactivity ("the influence of the researcher on the setting or individuals studied" [Maxwell, 1996, p. 91]) and researcher bias. Triangulation, like member checking, is a strategy that invites additional perspectives into the study to minimize the effect of these threats. Janesick (1994) reviews four types of triangulation identified by Denzin in 1978, and to these adds a fifth, as follows:

1. Data triangulation: the use of a variety of data sources in a study.
2. Investigator triangulation: the use of several different researchers or evaluators.
3. Theory triangulation: the use of multiple perspectives to interpret a single set of data.
4. Methodological triangulation: the use of multiple methods to study a single problem. (Kanter, 2006, pp. 105–106)

Triangulation Checklist

- ☐ Identify the forms of triangulation applied to confirm the findings.
- ☐ Identify how the forms of triangulation provided assurances of completeness of data.

TRUSTWORTHINESS FOR VERIFICATION

The researcher needs to provide an assurance that data were trustworthy if she or he conducted a qualitative study. In defining trustworthiness, the researcher demonstrates to the reader that the findings are consistent with those expressed by the study's participants. The researcher also describes the application of qualitative techniques that enhance data trustworthiness: reflexivity, audit trail, reduction of bias, triangulation, peer debriefing, member check, and prolonged engagement (Lietz, Langer, & Furman, 2006).

> A description of the research study's trustworthiness is located in the methodology chapter.

Example

In this example, the researcher describes the measures taken to ensure the trustworthiness of data collected in the study.

Measures to Ensure Trustworthiness

Having a strong structure for qualitative research, such as grounded theory, is just one of the critical components of sound qualitative research.

> This section explores trustworthiness and how that relates to the quality of the research. I explain specific measures that I took in my research to achieve a high level of trustworthiness.
>
> Trustworthiness is critical in order to ensure that research is sound. At the most basic level, trustworthiness is simply a way to ensure to the audience that the findings of the study are worthy of their trust and attention (Lincoln & Guba, 1985). Trustworthiness is the sign of well-designed and implemented qualitative research. Because traditional quantitative methods of controlling for internal and external validity, objectivity, and reliability are not appropriate to qualitative methods, Lincoln and Guba presented several criteria for trustworthiness that serve the same purpose in qualitative research. For this study, the methods I included were credibility, transferability, dependability, and confirmability. (Pepperell, 2006, p. 56)

Trustworthiness Checklist

- ☐ Identify how the study's findings reflect the participant's intent.
- ☐ Describe how each of the following was addressed to ensure trustworthiness: reflexivity, audit trail, reduction of bias, triangulation, peer debriefing, member check, and prolonged engagement.

TYPE OF DESIGN

The researcher identifies the type of research design and a rationale for its selection. The researcher first names the research design (e.g., qualitative, experimental, quasi-experimental, mixed methods, etc.). The researcher also describes how the research design chosen for the study is the most appropriate design to collect relevant data that address the study's research questions and hypotheses. The research design includes the specific research questions and hypotheses, methods, analysis, and quality of findings. The researcher's goal, regardless of research design chosen, is to demonstrate that the research design is objective; meets the tests for construct, internal, and external validity; is reliable; and demonstrates rigor and intellectual honesty (National Institute on Disability and Rehabilitation Research, 2008; Yin, 2003).

A description of the type of design is located in the methodology chapter.

Example

In this example, the researcher provides a clear description of the type of design used in the study. The researcher also provides a rationale for the use of this design.

The Type of Design

> The collective or cross-case study methodology provided a means of gathering data to consider teaching strategies and practices in inclusive classrooms. In this comparative case study, there were two stages of analysis: the within-case analysis and the cross-case analysis (Merriam, 1998). Within-case analysis entailed gathering data to get a comprehensive picture about the contextual variables that impacted each case. After analysis of each individual case was completed, cross-case analysis began. Cross-case analysis included comparing data from each case to find patterns in processes and outcomes that occurred across the cases, to understand how cases were qualified by contextual conditions, and to develop refined descriptions and powerful explanations (Miles & Huberman, 1994). This cross-case analysis provided a view of teachers in a suburban school district, teaching high school students in inclusive Algebra I classrooms. (Lowery, 2003, pp. 48–49)

Type of Design Checklist

- ☐ Be specific in naming the type of research design.
- ☐ Describe how the type of research design meets quality research standards.
- ☐ Describe how the type of research design meets the tests of construct, internal and external validity, and reliability.

U

UNITS OF ANALYSIS

The researcher describes the units of analysis. The units of analysis are the primary components being analyzed in the study (Trochim, 2006). The units of analysis may be a case, team, school, or individuals (De Vaus, 2001). The unit of analysis is the primary component from which the researcher collects data for analysis. The researcher provides the reader with a description of the unit of analysis, and, if using more than one unit of analysis, she or he describes the differences between the units of analysis (Babbie, 2004). Pay special attention not to draw conclusions from the wrong unit of analysis. This is known as the ecological fallacy (Richards, 1990).

> The units of analysis is first presented in the introductory chapter; a complete description of the units of analysis is located in the methodology chapter.

Example

In this example, the researcher describes the unit of analysis used in the study and presents a brief rationale for studying this unit of analysis.

Unit of Analysis

> The intent of Project REFRESH was to use multiple informants to capture the experiences of kin and nonkin foster families. The researchers collected data from foster parents, foster and birth children, as well as caseworkers. For the purpose of this study, examination of the data was

> limited to kin and nonkin foster parents only. The primary unit of analysis therefore is kin and nonkin foster parents. Because it may be valuable to understand family relationships as experienced by more than one family member (Bernard, 1972), the experience of foster children and birth children in the project should be examined. The perspectives of the caseworkers may also be informative. (De Costa, 2006, p. 91)

Units of Analysis Checklist

- ☐ The researcher links the units of analysis to the study's research questions and hypotheses.
- ☐ The researcher provides a description of the units of analysis that clearly states the "who" or "what" of the study.
- ☐ If the researcher uses more than one unit of analysis, she or he describes the differences between them.
- ☐ The units of analysis are the focus of the analysis.

V

VALIDITY

The researcher provides a description of how she or he ensured the validity of the study. Yin (2003) states that there are four tests that can be applied to gauge the quality of empirical research: construct validity, external validity, internal validity, and reliability. The researcher uses language consistent with his or her methodological approach (qualitative or quantitative) in the validation section that addresses construct validity, external validity, and internal validity. The researcher is careful not to define validity; she or he describes how the study met the standards for each of these aspects of validity.

> A description of the research study's validity is located in the methodology chapter.

Example

In this example, the researcher addresses issues of validity by describing how trustworthiness was achieved and how the pilot study added to the study's validity.

Validity

> Validity refers to the trustworthiness of a description or conclusion (Guba and Lincoln, 1981). In qualitative research, the strength of the research is that the case accurately describes and portrays the lived experience of those studied. I minimized problems of validity in this study by the length

of time of the interview and the depth of explanations given by participants. The purpose of this study was to gain an understanding of the participants' perceptions of school. Therefore, trustworthiness in this study refers to how I described and interpreted the words of the participants. One purpose of the pilot study I conducted was to ensure validity of the real study. Glesne (1999) describes the use of a pilot study to test several aspects of the proposed research. She says that the pilot study is done to learn about one's research process, observation techniques, and interview questions and to inform oneself about the research topic. (Carper, 2002, p. 46).

Validity Checklist

- ☐ Describe how content, external, and internal tests of validity were met.
- ☐ Provide sufficient detail to gauge the validity of the study.

VARIABLES

The researcher describes the variables in the study. The researcher may describe variables in several ways. Variables may be stated as independent or dependent variables. They may be stated as endogenous or exogenous. If the researcher is using an independent variable, she or he will describe how she or he manipulated the variable to cause an effect on the dependent variable—the dependent variable being the focus of the researcher's inquiry. If the researcher is not manipulating a variable in the study, she or he describes the relationship between and among the variables in the study (Price, 2000). The independent and dependent variable definition and example are listed under the appropriate heading.

> A description of the research study's variables is located in the methodology chapter.

Example

In this example, the researcher provides a definition for the types of variables used in this study.

Variables

> Contingency variables, such as environment, organizational size, task type, and task difficulty, put pressure on the organization to react by facing it with various levels of challenge that it must meet. Response variables are the actions that the organization takes to meet the requirements of the contingency variables, such as adopting a structure or strategy suitable to meet the challenge posed by the contingency variables. Performance variables refer to the results of adaptation to the contingencies, such as organizational effectiveness, survival, and growth. Contingency theory states that if the responses of the organization meet the requirements of the contingency variables, then organizational performance will be good (Drazin & Van de Ven, 1985; Van de Ven & Drazin, 1985). The degree to which the organization's responses match the demands of the contingencies is the degree of "fit" that the organization has achieved. (Cho, 2006, pp. 34–35)

Variables Checklist

- ☐ Identify the dependent and independent variables.
- ☐ Describe the manipulation of the independent variable on the dependent variable.
- ☐ Describe any relationship between or among variables if the study does not manipulate an independent variable.

VERIFICATION

The researcher uses the process of verification when replicating previously reported research. The researcher describes how she or he replicated research by applying a similar theoretical framework, research design, methodology, and data analysis. She or he uses the process of verification to substantiate previous research claims advancing the study's credibility, and adding to the line of inquiry. If the researcher's research does not replicate the original findings, the researcher describes the discrepancies in outcomes and indicates the need for further research. The researcher succinctly describes his or her rationale for the research, which is designed to verify previous research, citing the research, and describing its theoretical framework, methodology, data analysis, and findings (Grant, 2007).

> A description of the verification of the research study is presented in the findings and results or discussion chapters.

Example

In this example, the researcher describes the procedures used for verification of the study's data, advancing the study's credibility.

> ***Verification***
>
> Credibility
>
> Certain limitations are inevitable when one is dealing with a human data gathering and analyzing instrument—mistakes are made, opportunities are missed, and personal biases interfere (Merriam, 1988). Thus, credibility in qualitative methods "hinges to a great extent on the skill, competence, and rigor of the person doing fieldwork" (Patton, 1990, p. 14). In order to increase the credibility of results, procedures are implemented to verify the subjective interpretations of the researcher as a human data-gathering instrument. The following verification procedures were implemented throughout the qualitative evaluative case study of the Administrative Leadership Academy EYP: prolonged engagement and persistent observation, triangulation, and member checking (Glesne, 1999; Merriam, 1988). (Creasap, 2003, p. 85)

Verification Checklist

- ☐ The researcher presents an accurate description of the replicated research.
- ☐ The researcher describes the rationale for replicating the study.
- ☐ The researcher describes the process she or he used to ensure the integrity of the replication of the study.

VITA/VITAE (also Résumé)

Some dissertations require that the researcher's curriculum vita is included in the appendices. The curriculum vita, often referred to as a CV, presents the researcher's educational and academic credentials. The CV is written in rich detail providing both depth and breadth of the researcher's relevant experience. The CV offers accurate citations for publications, presentations, committee work, certificates and licenses, honors, awards, degrees, grants, and the researcher's role in work in progress. The researcher is careful to maintain the highest level of integrity in writing the CV.

The curriculum vita is placed in the appendices.

REFERENCES

Adams, J. (2007). Development and testing of an initial model of curricular leadership culture in middle schools. Unpublished doctoral dissertation, Texas Tech University, Lubbock, Texas.

Al-Washahi, M. (2007). The perceived effectiveness and impact of educational technology faculty development activities in the College of Education at Sultan Qaboos University. Unpublished doctoral dissertation, Ohio University, Athens, Ohio.

Ali, R. (2005). An analysis of transformational leadership exhibited by administrators of 1862 and 1890 cooperative extension programs in states with both systems as a predictor for the attainment of state match in Federal fiscal year 2004. Unpublished doctoral dissertation, Marshall University, Huntington, West Virginia.

American Psychological Association (2001). Publication manual of the American Psychological Association (5th ed.). Washington, DC: American Psychological Association.

Ates, C. (2003). The perceptions of African American community college presidents concerning their leadership styles and use of power. Unpublished doctoral dissertation, The University of Texas at Austin, Austin, Texas.

Babbie, E. (2004). The practice of social research. Belmont, CA: Wadsworth/Thomson Learning.

Bagozzi, R., Youjae, Y., & Phillips, L. (1991, September). Assessing construct validity in organizational research - includes appendices. Administrative Science Quarterly.

Bangert-Drowns, R. (2008). Guidelines for writing a doctoral dissertation. Retrieved August 6, 2008, from http://www.albany.edu/etap/graduate_programs/doctoral/Dissertation%20guidelines.doc.

Barringer, W. (2006). Leadership and learning: A comparative case study of leadership practices in two Washington state high schools. Unpublished doctoral dissertation, Washington State University, Pullman, Washington.

Batia, A. (2007). Relationships among personality, self-determination and exercise behavior. Unpublished doctoral dissertation, University of Florida, Gainesville, Florida.

Begley, C. (1996). Using triangulation in nursing research. Journal of Advanced Nursing, 24(1), 122–128.

Bennett, D. (2007). Teacher efficacy in the implementation of new curriculum supported by professional development. Unpublished doctoral dissertation, University of Montana, Missoula, Montana.

Berger, R., & Patchener, M. (1988). Implementing the research plan. London: Sage.

Bertrand, T. (2006). Cultural competence in evaluation: A black perspective. Unpublished doctoral dissertation, Florida State University, Tallahassee, Florida.

Black, T. (1999). Doing quantitative research in the social sciences: An integrated approach to research design, measurement and statistics. Thousand Oaks, CA: Sage.

Blumer, H. (1969). Symbolic interactionism: Perspective and method. Berkeley, CA: University of California Press.

Boehman, J. (2006). Affective, continuance, and normative commitment among student affairs professionals. Unpublished doctoral dissertation, North Carolina State University, Raleigh, North Carolina.

Boyd, K. (2004). An analysis of selected pre- and post-admission variables as they relate to the retention of new freshmen at a large, research, public university. Unpublished doctoral dissertation, Texas A & M University, College Station, Texas.

Brasfield, C. (2007). An exploration of the stressors, coping resources, and resiliency of rural mothers of children with special needs. Unpublished doctoral dissertation, Georgia State University, Atlanta, Georgia.

Brooks, M. (2007). Organizational leadership in academic libraries: Identifying culture types and leadership roles. Unpublished doctoral dissertation, Marshall University.

Brown, D. (2006). The role of pop culture based information and stereotypes versus direct knowledge of individuals in forming teacher expectations of African American students Unpublished doctoral dissertation, The University of North Carolina at Greensboro, Greensboro, North Carolina.

Brown, L. (2006). Using personality type to predict student success in a technology-rich classroom environment. Unpublished doctoral dissertation, North Carolina State University, Raleigh, North Carolina.

Burke, C. (2001, May 23). The doctoral dissertation proposal. Retrieved August 6, 2008, from http://www.usc.edu/schools/sppd/private/documents/doctoral/resources/dissertationproposal.pdf.

Burnette, M. (2006). The relationship between emotional intelligence of patrol sergeants and subordinate patrol officers. Unpublished doctoral dissertation, North Carolina State University, Raleigh, North Carolina.

Calabrese, R. (2006). The elements of an effective dissertation & thesis: A step-by-step guide to getting it right the first time. Lanham, MD: Rowman & Littlefield Education.

Campbell, M. (2003). The involvement of Florida's full-time community college faculty in institutional governance: Implications for institutional decision-making. Unpublished doctoral dissertation, University of South Florida, Tampa Bay, Florida.

Carpenter, P. (2006). Cyber connections across age and gender differences: How communication technologies enhance social communication in learning communities in online college courses. Unpublished doctoral dissertation, North Carolina State University, Raleigh, North Carolina.

Carper, A. (2002). Bright students in a wasteland: the at-risk gifted a qualitative study of fourteen gifted dropouts. Unpublished doctoral dissertation, North Carolina State University, Raleigh, North Carolina.

Cavins, B. (2005). The relationship between emotional-social intelligence and leadership practices among college student leaders. Unpublished doctoral dissertation, Bowling Green State University, Bowling Green, Ohio.

Champion, B. (2007). The effects of high-stakes testing on central office organizational culture: Changes in one school district. Unpublished doctoral dissertation, The University of Texas, Austin, Texas.

Charles-Liscombe, R. (2007). A national survey of athletic training educators' academic role strain, role orientation, and intent to leave. Unpublished doctoral dissertation, The University of North Carolina at Greensboro, Greensboro, North Carolina.

Chirume, E. (2008). A study of educational leadership: The principals' and teachers' perceptions of teacher leadership dynamics in Southeast Ohio. Unpublished doctoral dissertation, Ohio University, Athens, Ohio.

Cho, W. (2006). Contingency theory of group communication effectiveness in Korean organizations: Influence of fit between organizational structural variables and group relational climate on communication effectiveness. Unpublished doctoral dissertation, Texas A&M University, College Station, Texas.

Christian, T. (2008). A statewide evaluation of gifted education in Missouri. Unpublished doctoral dissertation, University of Missouri, Columbia, Missouri.

Clark, D., Guba, E., & Smith, G. (1977). Functions and definitions of functions of a research proposal. Indiana University.

Clark, N. (2005). Toward a construct validation of the Louisiana school analysis model instructional staff questionnaire. Unpublished doctoral dissertation, University of Louisiana, Baton Rouge, Louisiana.

Clinesmith, C. (2007). Access and use of meaningful research through transformational leadership: A collective-case study of public school principals. Unpublished doctoral dissertation, Texas Tech University, Lubbock, Texas.

Conde, J. (2006). Patterns of verbal communication in children with special needs. Unpublished doctoral dissertation, North Texas State University, Denton, Texas.

Constantino, S. (2002). High school student perspectives on the interaction between family involvement and peer relationships on their own school engagement practices. Unpublished doctoral dissertation, Virginia Polytechnic Institute and State University, Blacksburg, Virginia.

Council of the American Educational Research Association. (2006). Standards for reporting on empirical social science research in AERA publications. Educational Researcher, 35(6), 33–40.

Cox, D. (2004). Leaders fostering resiliency In schools. Unpublished doctoral dissertation, University of Pittsburgh, Pittsburgh, Pennsylvania.

Craig, T. (2007). ACT 1999-48 (24 P.S. Sections 12-1205.1 et seq.): An analysis of continuing professional education reform in Pennsylvania and implications for policy and practice. Unpublished doctoral dissertation, University of Pittsburgh, Pittsburgh, Pennsylvania.

Creasap, S. (2003). The effects of mentoring and sustained reflection on educational leadership practice: A case study of a novice principal and mentor participating in an administrative leadership academy. Unpublished doctoral dissertation, The Ohio State University, Columbus, Ohio.

Creswell, J. (2002). Research design. Thousand Oaks, CA: Sage.

Crim, S. (2006). African American eighth-grade female students' perceptions and experience as learners of science literacy. Unpublished doctoral dissertation, Georgia State University, Atlanta, Georgia.

Crocker, L. (2006). Introduction to measurement theory. In J. Green, G. Camilli, & P. Elmore (Eds.), Handbook of complementary methods in education research (pp. 371–384). Mahwah, NJ: Lawrence Erlbaum Associates.

Crotty, M. (2003). The foundations of social research. Thousand Oaks, CA: Sage.

Curran-Everett, D., & Benos, D. (2004). Guidelines for reporting statistics in journals published by the American Physiological Society. American Journal of Physiological, 287(2), 307–309.

Cybulski, T. (2003). Investigating the role of the collective efficacy of teachers in fiscal efficiency and student achievement. Unpublished doctoral dissertation, The Ohio State University, Columbus, Ohio.

Davies, C. (2005). A new democracy for professional development and research. Unpublished doctoral dissertation, Victoria University, Melbourne, Australia.

De Costa, J. (2006). An examination of kin and nonkin foster parents' experiences. Unpublished doctoral dissertation, Oregon State University, Corvallis, Oregon.

De Vaus, D. (2001). Research design in social research. Thousand Oaks, CA: Sage.

Deloatch-Anthony, L. (2005). Self-efficacy and work-readiness of disadvantaged females. Unpublished doctoral dissertation, University of Georgia at Athens, Athens, Georgia.

Denkinger, B. (2007). Research methods, the sequel: Psych 1001. Retrieved August 27, 2008, from http://www.psych.umn.edu/courses/fall07/denkingerb/psy1001pdfs/research_methods_2.pdf.

Dervin, B., & Reinhard, C. (2006). Researchers and practitioners talk about users and each other. Making user and audience studies matter—paper 1. Information Research, 12(1). Retrieved from http://inforationr.net/ir/12-1/paper286.html.

Dondanville, R. (2005). Assessing effective teacher behaviors in athletic training clinical education. Unpublished doctoral dissertation, The University of North Carolina at Greensboro, Greensboro, North Carolina.

Donnan, P. (2007). Conducting assessment online: Educational developers' perspectives. Unpublished doctoral dissertation, University of Wollongong, New South Wales, Australia.

Duckworth, M. (2008). Non-traditional public school superintendents: An exploratory case study. Unpublished doctoral dissertation, North Carolina State University, Raleigh, North Carolina.

Duncan, T. (2008). An analysis of the T.E.A.C.H. early childhood project: Factors related to perceptions of teachers' knowledge, skills and confidence. Unpublished doctoral dissertation, University of North Carolina at Chapel Hill, Chapel Hill, NC.

Duncon, D. (2004). School culture: Exploring its relationship with mental models and leadership behaviors In schools. Unpublished doctoral dissertation, Florida State University, Tallahassee, Florida.

Engel, R., & Schutt, R. (2005). The practice of research in social work. Thousand Oaks, CA: Sage.

Engle, M., Blumenthal, A., & Cosgrave, T. (2008). How to prepare an annotated bibliography. Retrieved August 4, 2008, from http://www.library.cornell.edu/olinuris/ref/research/skill28.htm.

Evaluation Research Team. (2008, December). Data collection methods for program evaluation: Observation. Evaluation Briefs, (16). Retrieved from http://www.cdc.gov/healthyYouth/evaluation/pdf/brief16.pdf.

Evans, M., Leake, D., McMullen, D., & Bogaerts, S. (2005). Contextual support for remote cooperative troubleshooting: Lessons from a naturalistic study. Paper presented at the 5th International Interdisciplinary Conference on Modelling and Using Context, Paris, France.

Gao, Z. (2007). Understanding students' motivation in physical education: Integration of expectancy-value model and self-efficacy theory. Unpublished doctoral dissertation, Louisiana State University and Agricultural and Mechanical College Baton Rouge, Louisiana.

Garson, G. D. (n.d.). Statnotes: Topics in multivariate analysis. Retrieved from http://www2.chass.ncsu.edu/garson/pa765/statnote.htm.

Gibaldi, J. (2003). MLA Handbook (6th ed.). New York: Modern Language Association.

Glaser, B., & Strauss, A. (1967). The discovery of grounded theory: Strategies for qualitative research. New Brunswick, NJ: Aldine Transaction.

Glasgow, J. (2008). An appreciative inquiry case study: Recognizing the positive core of teachers in a low SES elementary school that met standard of excellence. Unpublished doctoral dissertation, Wichita State University, Wichita, Kansas.

Goedde, A. (2006). Factors predicting preservice teacher technology competency. Unpublished doctoral dissertation, Bowling Green State University, Bowling Green, Ohio.

Gogus, C. (2005). Recipient allocation preferences and organizational choices: A fit perspective. Unpublished doctoral dissertation, Texas A&M University, College Station, Texas.

Gonzales, J. (2006). The acculturation experience of international graduate students: A qualitative investigation. Unpublished doctoral dissertation, University of Notre Dame, Notre Dame, Indiana.

Grant, J. (2007). Verifying evidence of "Congressional Enactments of Race-Gender." Retrieved July 2, 2009, from http://polmeth.wustl.edu/retrieve@php?id=687.

Gross, M. (2006). Instructional design thought processes of expert nurse educators. Unpublished doctoral dissertation, Virginia Polytechnic Institute and State University, Blacksburg, Virginia.

Guba, E., & Lincoln, Y. (1981). Effective evaluations. San Francisco, CA: Jossey-Bass.

Haig, B. (1995). Grounded theory as scientific method. Unpublished manuscript.

Hathorn, D. (2006). Lived experience of nurses working with student nurses in the acute care clinical environment. Unpublished doctoral dissertation, Louisiana State University and Agricultural and Mechanical College, Baton Rouge, Louisiana.

Hayes III, S. (2007). Principal and teacher beliefs and knowledge regarding grade retention: A case study. Unpublished doctoral dissertation, University of Missouri, Columbia, Missouri.

Heffner, C. (2004). Research methods. Retrieved from http://allpsych.com/researchmethods/validityreliability.html.

Henderson, D. (2007). The leadership triad: Identity-integrity-authenticity a case study of the inner life and leadership of educational leaders. Unpublished doctoral dissertation, University of Montana, Missoula, Montana.

Hershey, D., Jacobs-Lawson, J., & Wilson, T. (2005). Research as a script. In F. Leong & J. Austin (Eds.), The psychology research handbook: A guide for graduate students and research assistants (2nd ed., pp. 3–22). Thousand Oaks, CA: Sage.

Hill, P. (2005). Addiction and recovery experiences of African American women: A phenomenological study. Unpublished doctoral dissertation, Virginia Commonwealth University, Richmond, Virginia.

Hodum, T. (2007). An investigation of how students, faculty, and administrators within a particular liberal arts college perceived a new-student orientation program's effect on students' social integration and retention. Unpublished doctoral dissertation, University of Missouri at Columbia, Columbia, Missouri.

Holosko, M. (2001). Overview of qualitative research methods. In B. Thyer (Ed.), The handbook of social work research methods (pp. 263–271). Thousand Oaks, CA: Sage.

Howell, J., Miller, P., Park, H., Sattler, D., Schack, T., Sery, E., et al. (2005). Reliability and validity. Writing@CSU. Retrieved August 12, 2008, from http://writing.colostate.edu/guides/research/relval/com2b4.cfm.

Hughes, W. (2001). What makes a good research paper? ARCOM Newsletter, 16(3), 1–4.

Hummel, C. (2007). Using appreciative inquiry to describe and create teacher peak experiences: A case study of elementary school teachers. Unpublished doctoral dissertation, Wichita State University, Wichita, Kansas.

Jaffe, C. (2006). Multiple perspectives on Georgia's early intervention program: A qualitative inquiry. Unpublished doctoral dissertation, Georgia State University, Atlanta, Georgia.

Jarvelin, K., & Wilson, T. (2003). On conceptual models for information seeking and retrieval research. Information Research, 9(1), 163. Retrieved from http://informationr.net/ir/9-1/paper163.html.

Johnson, H. (2004). Individual perceptions of leadership attributes by industrial technology teachers in selected public high and technical high schools in Jamaica. Unpublished doctoral dissertation, North Carolina State University, Raleigh, North Carolina.

Jung, S. (2006). Understanding racial-ethnic disparities in internal school suspension and identifying compensatory and protective factors. Unpublished doctoral dissertation, The University of Texas, Austin, Texas.

Kanter, S. (2006). Embodying research: A study of student engagement in research writing Unpublished doctoral dissertation, Indiana University of Pennsylvania, Indiana, Pennsylvania.

Kerlinger, F. (1979). Behavioral research: A conceptual approach. New York: Holt, Rinehart, & Winston.

Kessler, F. (2008). Understanding descriptive statistics. Retrieved from http://www.nationalatlas.gov/articles/mapping/a_statistics.html.

Kimmel, A. (1988). Ethics and values in applied social research. Thousand Oaks, CA: Sage.

Kitchener, K. (2000). Foundations of ethical practice, research, and teaching in psychology. Mahwah, NJ: Lawrence Erlbaum Associates.

Knapik, G. (2006). Being delivered: Spirituality in survivors of sexual violence. Unpublished doctoral dissertation, Kent State University, Kent, Ohio.

Krumme, G. (2000). Phases, stages, and steps in geographic investigation & research. Retrieved December 6, 2005, from http://faculty.washington.edu/~krumme/guides/researchguide.html#frame.

Lenth, R. (2001). Some practical guidelines for effective sample-size determination (No. 303). Iowa City, IA: University of Iowa.

Lien, L. (2002). The role of social integration in students' psychosocial development. Unpublished doctoral dissertation, Vanderbilt University, Nashville, Tennessee.

Lietz, C., Langer, C., & Furman, R. (2006). Establishing trustworthiness in qualitative research in social work. Qualitative Social Work, 5(4), 441–458.

Loop, P. (1997). Case studies of exemplary elementary school guidance programs in southwest Virginia, Unpublished doctoral dissertation, Virginia Polytechnic Institute and State University, Blacksburg, Virginia.

Lowery, L. (2003). Instructional strategies and practices used to enhance student success in the high school algebra I inclusive classroom. Unpublished doctoral dissertation, Virginia Polytechnic Institute and State University, Blacksburg, Virginia.

Ma, Y. (2006). Exploring faculty perceptions of a case library as an online teaching resource. Unpublished doctoral dissertation, Georgia State University, Atlanta, Georgia.

Magone, M. (2007). Education law priorities and need: A comparative analysis. Unpublished doctoral dissertation, University of Montana, Missoula, Montana.

Maher, M. (2004). An investigation of teacher candidate ethical identity. Unpublished doctoral dissertation, North Carolina State University, Raleigh, North Carolina.

Mangino, J. (2008). Voices of teen mothers: Their challenges, support systems, and successes. Unpublished doctoral dissertation, University of Pittsburgh, Pittsburgh, Pennsylvania.

Marczyk, G., DeMatteo, D., & Festinger, D. (2005). Essentials of research design and methodology. Hoboken, NJ: John Wiley and Sons.

Martin, T. (2006). Information processing and college choice: An examination of recruitment information on higher education web sites using the heuristic-systematic model. Unpublished doctoral dissertation, Florida State University, Tallahassee, Florida.

McCoy, D. (2006). Entering the academy: Exploring the socialization experiences of African American male faculty. Unpublished doctoral dissertation, Louisiana State University, Baton Rouge, Louisiana.

McGaghie, W., & Crandall, S. (2001). Data analysis and statistics. Academic Medicine, 76(9), 936–938.

McIntosh, C. (2006). Does a day make a difference? A comparison of half-day and full-day kindergarten programs in two Ohio school districts. Unpublished doctoral dissertation, Miami University, Oxford, Ohio.

Merriam, S. (2001). Qualitative research and case study applications in education (2nd ed.). San Francisco, CA: Jossey-Bass.

Miles, M., & Huberman, A. (1994). Qualitative data analysis: An expanded sourcebook (2nd ed.). Thousand Oaks, CA: Sage.

Moher, D. (2007). Reporting research results: A moral obligation for all researchers. Canadian Journal of Anesthesia, 54, 331–335.

Mombourquette, C. (2007). Involvement and high school student engagement, academic achievement, attendance, and attitude toward school. Unpublished doctoral dissertation, The University of Montana, Missoula, Montana.

Moore, J. (2006). Adequate yearly progress: Leaving explanation behind? Unpublished doctoral dissertation, Mississippi State University, Mississippi State, Mississippi.

Moore, M. (1997). Connecting school-based learning and work-based learning perceptions of students, their teachers, and their workplace supervisors. Unpublished doctoral dissertation, Virginia Polytechnic Institute and State University, Blacksburg, Virginia.

Moore Morton, C. (1999). Executive directors at research and doctoral I universities in the next decade. Unpublished doctoral dissertation, Virginia Polytechnic Institute and State University, Blacksburg, Virginia.

Mulligan, G. (2005). The participation of language minority families in formal school activities. Unpublished doctoral dissertation, University of Notre Dame, Notre Dame, Indiana.

Myers, M. (1997). Qualitative research in information systems. MIS Quarterly, 21(2), 241–242. Retrieved from http://www.misq.org/discovery/MISQD_isworld/.

National Institute of Child Health and Human Development. (2008). Steps involved in clinical research efforts. Retrieved September 22, 2008, from http://www.nichd.nih.gov/health/clinicalresearch/steps/develop_implement.cfm.

National Institute on Disability and Rehabilitation Research. (2008). What are the standards for quality research (No. 9). Washington, DC: U.S. Department of Education.

Neto-Sydenstricker, J. (1997). Research design and mixed-method approach: A hands-on experience. Retrieved August 19, 2008, from http://www.socialresearchmethods.net/tutorial/Sydenstricker/bolsa.html.

Neville, E. (2006). A case study of social studies curriculum for inclusion of multicultural education. Unpublished doctoral dissertation, University of Missouri at Columbia, Columbia, Missouri.

Niles, R. (2006). A study of the application of emerging technology: Teacher and student perceptions of the impact of one-to-one laptop computer access. Unpublished doctoral dissertation, Wichita State University, Wichita, Kansas.

Nokdee, S. (2007). Self-directed learning among Thai nurses in clinical practice. Unpublished doctoral dissertation, Victoria University, Victoria, Australia.

O'Connor, T. (2006). MagaLinks in criminal justice. Retrieved August 25, 2008, from http://www.apsu.edu/oconnort/3760/3760lect03.htm.

O'Grady, K. (2006). The role of inspiration in scientific scholarship and discovery: Views of theistic scientists. Unpublished doctoral dissertation, Brigham Young University, Salt Lake City, Utah.

Office of Behavioral and Social Sciences Research. (2001). Qualitative methods in health research. In National Institute of Health (Ed.). Washington, DC: National Institute of Health.

Office of Research Integrity. (2007, January). Guidelines for responsible conduct of research. In University of Pittsburgh (Ed.), Office of Research Integrity. Pittsburgh, Pennsylvania.

Oxford Reference Online. (2007). Confounding. In J. Last (Eds.), A dictionary of public health. Available from http://www.oxfordreference.com.proxy.lib.ohio-state.edu/views/ENTRY.html?subview=Main&entry=t235.e877.

Parker, D. (2007). Navigating the social/cultural politics of school choice: Why do parents choose Montessori? A case study. Unpublished doctoral dissertation, The University of North Carolina at Greensboro, Greensboro, North Carolina.

Patton, M. Q. (2002). Qualitative research & evaluation methods (3rd ed.). Thousand Oaks: Sage.

Payne, D. (2007). Exploring the importance of geographic place for adolescent well-being: Influences on violence, pregnancy views, and academic achievement. Unpublished doctoral dissertation, The Ohio State University, Columbus, Ohio.

Pedraza, L. (2006). "Because they are spiritually discerned": Spirituality in early childhood education. Unpublished doctoral dissertation, The Ohio State University, Columbus, Ohio.

Pepperell, J. (2006). The experience of gifted girls transitioning from elementary school to sixth and seventh grade. Unpublished doctoral dissertation, Oregon State University, Corvallis, Oregon.

Polgar, S., & Thomas, S. (2000). Introduction to research in the health sciences. Philadelphia, PA: Elsevier Health Sciences.

Price, I. (2000). Behavioural science and research. Retrieved September 26, 2008, from http://www.une.edu.au/WebStat/unit_materials/c1_behavioural_science_research/index.html.

Richards, J. (1990). Units of analysis and the individual differences fallacy in environmental assessment. Environment and Behavior, 22(3), 307–319.

Rider, P. (2006). The interaction of peer influence and self-presentation in college students' alcohol consumption. Unpublished doctoral dissertation, University of Maryland College Park, College Park, Maryland.

Roberts, S. (2006). Teacher collaboration and elementary science teaching: Using action research as a tool for instructional leadership. Unpublished doctoral dissertation, The University of North Carolina at Greensboro, Greensboro, North Carolina.

Robinson, W. (2007). Operational definitions. Retrieved August 27, 2008, from http://web.utk.edu/~wrobinso/540_lec_opdefs.html.

Romancnuk, J. (2006). Implementation of a special education parent advisory committee: A mixed methods investigation into the members' experience of parental involvement with the school system. Unpublished doctoral dissertation, The University of Tennessee, Knoxville, Tennessee.

Roy, R. (2004). A grounded theory approach to the extension and revision of Scanlan's sport commitment model. Unpublished doctoral dissertation, Simon Fraser, Burnaby, British Columbia, Canada.

Rubin, A., & Babbie, E. (2004). Research methods for social work. Belmont, CA: Thomson Wadsworth.

Russell Berry, B. (2004). Succession to school leadership: Challenge and response for principals. Unpublished doctoral dissertation, Texas A&M University, College Station, Texas.

Rysz, T. (2004). Metacognition in learning elementary probability and statistics. Unpublished doctoral dissertation, University of Cincinnati, Cincinnati, Ohio.

San Martin, T. (2008). Empowering students to enhance pedagogy: An appreciative inquiry case study of alternative high school students' high point learning experiences. Unpublished doctoral dissertation, Wichita State University, Wichita, Kansas.

Sanders, K. (2008). The relationship of selected academic factors to the persistence of general education development (GED) recipients enrolled in community colleges: An Oregon study. Oregon State University, Corvallis, Oregon.

Schensul, J., LeCompte, M., & Schensul, S. (1999). The ethnographer's toolkit. Lanham, MD: Altamira.

Schulz, B. (2005). Teachers' perspectives of how high-stakes testing influences instructional decisions and professionalism. Unpublished doctoral dissertation, University of Georgia Athens, Athens, Georgia.

Seagraves, J. (2007). "I don't think about being a black student and going through school": An exploration into the development of academic identity in African American students. Unpublished doctoral dissertation, The University of North Carolina at Greensboro, Greensboro, North Carolina.

Senholzi, M. (2005). The validation and generalization of the work attitudes and behaviors inventory (WABI). Unpublished doctoral dissertation, Florida State University, Tallahassee, Florida.

Sheehy, L. (2007). Leadership for co-teaching: A distributed perspective. Unpublished doctoral dissertation, Virginia Polytechnic Institute and State University, Blacksburg, Virginia.

Sheppard, D. (2007). Understanding how highly involved minority parents sustain their involvement in their child's education. Unpublished doctoral dissertation, Wichita State University, Wichita, Kansas.

Skelton, J., & Edwards, S. (2000). The function of the discussion section in academic medical writing. British Medical Journal, 320(7244), 1269–1270.

Smith, J. (2004). Assessing prospective students for master's level CACRP counseling programs: Evaluation of personal-emotional characteristics. Unpublished doctoral dissertation, Blacksburg, Virginia.

Smothers, R. (2004). The influence of state merit-based aid on access and educational experiences: An exploration of the Louisiana tuition opportunity program for students (TOPS). Unpublished doctoral dissertation, Louisiana State University and Agricultural and Mechanical College, Baton Rouge, Louisiana.

Somani, I. (2008). Inculturation and aculturation use of television among Asian Indians in the U.S. Unpublished doctoral dissertation, University of Maryland College Park, College Park, Maryland.

Sparks, K. (2005). The effect of teacher certification on student achievement. Unpublished doctoral dissertation, Texas A&M University, College Station, Texas.

Stalions, E. (2007). Dynamic criteria mapping: A study of the rhetorical values of placement evaluators. Unpublished doctoral dissertation, Bowling Green State University, Bowling Green, Ohio.

Sumner, M. (2006). Climate and student performance in Tennessee middle schools. Unpublished doctoral dissertation, The University of Tennessee, Knoxville, Tennessee.

Suprina, J. (2005). Using life-style and coping resources to differentiate between gay men with and without alcohol problems: An Adlerian study. Unpublished doctoral dissertation, Georgia State College, Atlanta, Georgia.

Taniguchi, S. (2004). Outdoor education and meaningful learning: Finding the attributes of meaningful learning experience in an outdoor education program. Unpublished doctoral dissertation, Brigham Young University, Salt Lake City, Utah.

Taylor, D., & Procter, M. (2008). The literature review: A few tips on conducting it. Retrieved August 21, 2008, from http://www.utoronto.ca/writing/litrev.html.

Teachey, A. (2003). Investigations in conceptual understanding of polynomial functions and the impact of mathematical belief systems on achievement in an accelerated summer program for gifted students. Unpublished doctoral dissertation, North Carolina State University, Raleigh, North Carolina.

Thompson, C. (2007). A multi-case examination of the impact of national board certification on the profession of teaching. Unpublished doctoral dissertation, University of Missouri, Columbia, Missouri.

Trochim, W. (2001). The research methods knowledge base (2nd ed.). Cincinnati, OH: Atomic Dog.

Trochim, W. (2006). Research methods knowledge base. Mason, OH: Atomic Dog.

Tull, A. (2004). The relationship between perceived level of synergistic supervision received, job satisfaction, and intention to turnover of new professionals in student affairs administration. Unpublished doctoral dissertation, Florida State University, Tallahassee, Florida.

U.S. Department of Health and Human Services. (2005). Protection of human subjects (45 C.F.R. § 46.102 [f] [2]). Washington, DC: Government Printing Office.

U.S. Environmental Protection Agency. (2008). Research strategies. Retrieved September 23, 2008, from http://www.epa.gov/ORD/htm/researchstrategies.htm.

Vanhook-Morrissey, S. (2003). Female community college presidents' career development processes: A qualitative analysis. Unpublished doctoral dissertation, North Carolina State University, Raleigh, North Carolina.

Vyortkina, D. (2003). Portfolio assessment in educational leadership programs at master's level. Unpublished doctoral dissertation, Florida State University, Tallahassee, Florida.

Wede, J. (1996). Teacher selection: Use of demonstration lessons. Unpublished doctoral dissertation, Drake University, Des Moines, Iowa.

West, S. (2002). Development of an instrument to assess residents' perceptions of equity. Unpublished doctoral dissertation, Texas A&M University, College Station, Texas.

White, M. (2002). Making the transition from paraeducator to professional educator: Five minority teachers share their stories. Unpublished doctoral dissertation, Virginia Polytechnic Institute and State University Blacksburg, Virginia.

Witt, H. (2003). An examination of how educational administration programs prepare principals in special education issues. Unpublished doctoral dissertation, University of Cincinnati, Cincinnati, Ohio.

Wojtalewicz, M. (2004). Examination of head start children's social competence and social cognitions after participating in a universal violence prevention program. Unpublished doctoral dissertation, University of Florida, Gainesville, Florida.

Writing Centre. (2006). Writing in the sciences. Retrieved August 21, 2008, from http://www.queensu.ca/writingcentre/handouts/writing%20in%20the%20sciences.pdf.

Yin, R. (2003). Case study research: Design and methods (3rd ed.). Thousand Oaks, CA: Sage.

Zaman, H. (2006). Teachers' perceptions of citizenship and citizenship education: A comparative study. Unpublished doctoral dissertation, University of Pittsburgh, Pittsburgh, Pennsylvania.

ABOUT THE AUTHOR

Raymond L. Calabrese is professor of educational administration in the School of Educational Leadership and Policy at The Ohio State University. He is leading the development of the first Ed.D. at The Ohio State University. He has a rich background across K-12 and higher education and is known as an academic scholar. He works nationally with faculty and students to enhance dissertation completion and is the author or coauthor of seven scholarly books. He has published over one hundred refereed journal articles in educational journals. He has received honors for his teaching, research, and publications. He can be contacted at calabrese.31@osu.edu.

21581814R00114

Printed in Great Britain
by Amazon